# PERSONS AND NUMBERS.

The person and number of a verb are those modifications in which it agrees with its subject or nominative.

In each number, there are three persons; and in each person, two numbers: thus,

*Singular. Plural.* 1st per. I love, 1st per. We love, 2d per. Thou lovest, 2d per. You love, 3d per. He loves; 3d per. They love.

Definitions universally applicable have already been given of all these things; it is therefore unnecessary to define them again in this place.

Where the verb is varied, the second person singular is regularly formed by adding *st* or *est* to the first person; and the third person singular, in like manner, by adding *s* or *es*: as, I *see*, thou *seest*, he *sees*; I *give*, thou *givest*, he *gives*; I *go*, thou *goest*, he *goes*; I *fly*, thou *fliest*, he *flies*; I *vex*, thou *vexest*, he *vexes*; I *lose*, thou *losest*, he *loses*.

Where the verb is not varied to denote its person and number, these properties are inferred from its subject or nominative: as, If I *love*, if thou *love*, if he *love*; if we *love*, if you *love*, if they *love*.

**OBSERVATIONS.**

OBS. 1.—It is considered a principle of Universal Grammar, that a finite verb must agree with its subject or nominative in person and number. Upon this principle, we ascribe to every such verb the person and number of the nominative word, whether the verb itself be literally modified by the relation or not. The doctrine must be constantly taught and observed, in every language in which the verbs have *any variations* of this kind. But suppose an instance, of a language in which all the verbs were entirely destitute of such inflections; the principle, as regards that language, must drop. Finite verbs, in such a case, would still relate to their subjects, or nominatives, agreeably to the sense; but they would certainly be rendered incapable of adding to this relation any agreement or disagreement. So the concords which belong to adjectives and participles in Latin and Greek, are rejected in English, and there remains to these parts of speech nothing but a simple relation to their nouns according to the sense. And by the fashionable substitution of *you* for *thou*, the concord of English verbs with their nominatives, is made to depend, in common practice, on little more than one single terminational *s*, which is used to mark one person of one number of one tense of one mood of each verb. So near does this practice bring us to the dropping of what is yet called a universal principle of grammar.[235]

OBS. 2.—In most languages, there are in each tense, through all the moods of every verb, six different terminations to distinguish the different persons and numbers. This will be well understood by every one who has ever glanced at the verbs as exhibited in any Latin, Greek, French, Spanish, or Italian grammar. To explain it to others, a brief example shall be given: (with the remark, that the Latin pronouns, here inserted, are seldom expressed, except for emphasis:) "*Ego amo*, I love; *Tu amas*, Thou lovest; *Ille amat*, He loves; *Nos amamus*, We love; *Vos amatis*, You love; *Illi amant*, They love." Hence it may be perceived, that the paucity of variations in the English verb, is a very striking peculiarity of our language.

# Unlock Your Language Potential

# SpeakUp English Grammar Language

William K. Spier

3 8002 02603 593 3

Whether we are gainers or losers by this simplicity, is a question for learned idleness to discuss. The common people who speak English, have far less inclination to add new endings to our verbs, than to drop or avoid all the remains of the old. Lowth and Murray tell us, "This scanty provision of terminations *is sufficient* for all the purposes of discourse;" and that, "*For this reason*, the plural termination *en*, (they *loven*, they *weren*,) formerly in use, was laid aside as *unnecessary*, and has long been obsolete."—*Lowth's Gram.*, p. 31; *Murray's*, 63.

OBS. 3.—Though modern usage, especially in common conversation, evidently inclines to drop or shun all unnecessary suffixes and inflections, still it is true, that the English verb in some of its parts, varies its termination, to distinguish, or agree with, the different persons and numbers. The change is, however, principally confined to the second and third persons singular of the present tense of the indicative mood, and to the auxiliaries *hast* and *has* of the perfect. In the ancient biblical style, now used only on solemn occasions, the second person singular is distinguished through all the tenses of the indicative and potential moods. And as the use of the pronoun *thou* is now mostly confined to the solemn style, the terminations of that style are retained in connexion with it, through all the following examples of the conjugation of verbs. In the plural number, there is no variation of ending, to denote the different persons; and the verb in the three persons plural, (with the two exceptions *are* and *were*, from *am* and *was*,) is the same as in the first person singular. Nor does the use of *you* for the singular, warrant its connexion with any other than the plural form of the verb. This strange and needless confusion of the numbers, is, in all languages that indulge it, a practical inconvenience. It would doubtless have been much better, had *thou* and *you* still kept their respective places—the one, nominative singular—the other, objective plural—as they appear in the Bible. But as the English verb is always attended by a noun or a pronoun, expressing the subject of the affirmation, no ambiguity arises from the want of particular terminations in the verb, to distinguish the different persons and numbers.

OBS. 4.—Although our language, in its ordinary use, exhibits the verbs in such forms only, as will make, when put together, but a very simple conjugation; there is probably no other language on earth, in which it would be so difficult for a learned grammarian to fix, settle, and exhibit, to the satisfaction of himself and others, the principles, paradigms, rules, and exceptions, which are necessary for a full and just exhibition of this part of speech. This difficulty is owing, partly to incompatibilities or unsettled boundaries between the solemn and the familiar style; partly to differences in the same style between ancient usage and modern; partly to interfering claims of new and old forms of the preterit and the perfect participle; partly to the conflicting notions of different grammarians respecting the subjunctive mood; and partly to the blind tenacity with which many writers adhere to rugged derivatives, and prefer unutterable contractions to smooth and easy abbreviations. For example: a clergyman says to a lucky gamester, (1.) "*You dwell* in a house which *you* neither *planned* nor *built*." A member of the Society of Friends would say, (2.) "*Thou dwellst* in a house which *thou* neither *planned* nor *built*." Or, if not a scholar, as likely as not, (3.) "*Thee dwells* in a house which *thee* neither *planned* nor *built*." The old or solemn style would b3, (4.) "*Thou dwellest* in a house which *thou* neither *plannedst* nor *buildedst*." Some untasteful and overgrammatical poet will have it, (5.) "*Thou dwell'st* in halls *thou* neither *plann'dst* nor *build'dst*." The doctrine of Murray's Grammar, and of most others, would require, (6.) "*Thou dwellest* in a house which *thou* neither *plannedst* nor *builtest*." Or, (according to this author's method of avoiding unpleasant sounds,) the more complex form, (7.) "*Thou dost dwell* in a house which *thou* neither *didst plan* nor *didst build*." Out of these an other poet will make the line, (8.) "*Dost dwell* in halls which *thou* nor *plann'dst* nor *built'st*." An other, more tastefully, would drop the *st* of the preterit, and contract the present, as in the second instance above: thus,

> (9.) "*Thou dwellst* in halls *thou* neither *planned* nor *built,* And *revelst* there in riches won by guilt."

OBS. 5.—Now let all these nine different forms of saying the same thing, by the same verbs, in the same mood, and the same two tenses, be considered. Let it also be noticed, that for these same verbs within these limits, there are yet other forms, of a complex kind; as, "*You do dwell,*" or, "*You are dwelling;*" used in lieu of, "*Thou dost dwell,*" or, "*Thou art dwelling:*" so, "*You did plan,*" or, "*You were planning;*" used in lieu of, "*Thou didst plan,*" or, "*Thou wast planning.*" Take into the account the opinion of Dr. Webster and others, that, "*You was planning,*" or, "*You was building,*" is a still better form for the singular number; and well "established by national usage, both here and in England."—*Improved Gram.*, p. 25. Add the less inaccurate practice of some, who use *was* and *did* familiarly with *thou*; as, "*Thou was planning, did thou build?*" Multiply all this variety tenfold, with a view to the other moods and tenses of these three verbs, *dwell*, *plan*, and *build*; then extend the product, whatever it is, from these three common words, to *all* the verbs in the English language. You will thus begin to have some idea of the difficulty mentioned in the preceding observation. But this is only a part of it; for all these things relate only to the second person singular of the verb. The double question is, Which of these forms ought to be approved and taught for that person and number? and which of them ought to be censured and rejected as bad English? This question is perhaps as important, as any that can arise in English grammar. With a few candid observations by way of illustration, it will be left to the judgement of the reader.

OBS. 6.—The history of *youyouing* and *thoutheeing* appears to be this. Persons in high stations, being usually surrounded by attendants, it became, many centuries ago, a species of court flattery, to address individuals of this class, in the plural number, as if a great man were something more than one person. In this way, the notion of greatness was agreeably *multiplied*, and those who laid claim to such honour, soon began to think themselves insulted whenever they were addressed with any other than the plural pronoun.[236] Humbler people yielded through fear of offence; and the practice extended, in time, to all ranks of society: so that at present the customary mode of familiar as well as complimentary address, is altogether plural; both the verb and the pronoun being used in that form.[237] This practice, which confounds one of the most important distinctions of the language, affords a striking instance of the power of fashion. It has made propriety itself *seem* improper. But shall it be allowed, in the present state of things, to confound our conjugations and overturn our grammar? Is it right to introduce it into our paradigms, as the only form of the second person singular, that modern usage acknowledges? Or is it expedient to augment by it that multiplicity of other forms, which must either take this same place or be utterly rejected? With due deference to those grammarians who have adopted one or the other of these methods, the author of this work answers all these questions decidedly in the negative. It is not to be denied, that the use of the plural *for the singular* is now so common as to form the *customary mode* of address to individuals of every rank. The Society of Friends, or Quakers, however, continue to employ the singular number in familiar discourse; and custom, which has now destroyed the compliment of the plural, has removed also the supposed opprobrium of the singular, and placed it on an equality with the plural in point of respect. The singular is universally employed in reference to the Supreme Being; and is generally preferred in poetry. It is the language of Scripture, and of the Prayer-Book;

and is consistently retained in nearly all our grammars; though not always, perhaps, consistently treated.

OBS. 7.—Whatever is fashionable in speech, the mere disciples of fashion will always approve; and, probably, they will think it justifiable to despise or neglect all that is otherwise. These may be contented with the sole use of such forms of address as, "*You, you, sir;*"—"*You, you, madam.*" But the literati who so neglect all the services of religion, as to forget that these are yet conducted in English independently of all this fashionable youyouing, must needs be poor judges of what belongs to their own justification, either as grammarians or as moral agents. A fashion by virtue of which millions of youths are now growing up in ignorance of that form of address which, in their own tongue, is most appropriate to poetry, and alone adapted to prayer, is perhaps not quite so light a matter as some people imagine. It is at least so far from being a good reason for displacing that form from the paradigms of our verbs in a grammar, that indeed no better needs be offered for tenaciously retaining it. Many children may thus learn at school what all should know, and what there is little chance for them to learn elsewhere. Not all that presume to minister in religion, are well acquainted with what is called the solemn style. Not all that presume to explain it in grammars, do know what it is. A late work, which boasted the patronage of De Witt Clinton, and through the influence of false praise came nigh to be imposed by a law of New York on all the common schools of that State; and which, being subsequently sold in Philadelphia for a great price, was there republished under the name of the "National School Manual;" gives the following account of this part of grammar: "In the solemn and poetic styles, the second person singular, in both the above tenses, is thou; and the second person plural, is ye, *or you.* The verb, to agree with the second person singular, changes its termination. Thus: 2d person, sing. Pres. Tense, Thou walkest, *or Thou walketh.* Imperfect Tense, Thou walkedst. In the third person singular, *in the above styles,* the verb has sometimes *a different* termination; as, Present Tense, He, she, or *it walks* or walketh. The *above form of inflection* may be applied *to all verbs* used in the solemn *or* poetic *styles*; but for ordinary purposes, I have supposed it proper to employ the form of the verb, adopted in common conversation, as least perplexing to young minds."—*Bartlett's Common School Manual*, Part ii, p. 114. What can be hoped from an author who is ignorant enough to think "*Thou walketh*" is good English? or from one who tells us, that "*It walks*" is of the solemn style? or from one who does not know that *you* is never a *nominative* in the style of the Bible?

OBS. 8.—Nowhere on earth is fashion more completely mistress of all the tastes and usages of society, than in France. Though the common French Bible still retains the form of the second person singular, which in that language is shorter and perhaps smoother than the plural; yet even that sacred book, or at least the New Testament, and that by different persons, has been translated into more fashionable French, and printed at Paris, and also at New York, with the form of address everywhere plural; as, "Jesus anticipated him, saying, 'What *do you think*, Simon? of whom do the kings of the earth take taxes and tribute?'"—*Matt.*, xvii, 24. "And, going to prayers, they said, '0 Lord, *you who know* the hearts of all men, show which of these two *you have chosen.*'"—*Acts*, i, 24. This is one step further in the progress of politeness, than has yet been taken in English. The French grammarians, however, as far as I can perceive, have never yet disturbed the ancient order of their conjugations and declensions, by inserting the plural verb and pronoun in place of the singular; and, in the familiarity of friendship, or of domestic life, the practice which is denominated *tutoyant,* or *thoutheeing,* is far more prevalent in France than in England. Also, in the prayers of the French, the second person singular appears to be yet generally preserved, as it is in those of the English and the Americans. The less frequent use of it in the familiar conversation of the latter, is very probably owing to the general impression, that it cannot be used with propriety, except in the solemn style. Of this matter, those who have laid it aside themselves, cannot with much modesty pretend to judge for those who have not; or, if they may, there is still a question how far it is right to lay it aside. The following lines are a sort of translation from Horace; and I submit it to the reader, whether it is comely for a Christian divine to be less reverent toward God, than a heathen poet; and whether the plural language here used, does not lack the reverence of the original, which is singular:—

"Preserve, Almighty Providence!
Just what *you gave* me, competence."—*Swift*.

OBS. 9.—The terms, *solemn style, familiar style, modern style, ancient style, legal style, regal style, nautic style, common style*, and the like, as used in grammar, imply no certain divisions of the language; but are designed merely to distinguish, in a general way, the *occasions* on which some particular forms of expression may be considered proper, or the *times* to which they belong. For what is grammatical sometimes, may not be so always. It would not be easy to tell, definitely, in what any one of these styles consists; because they all belong to one language, and the number or nature of the peculiarities of each is not precisely fixed. But whatever is acknowledged to be peculiar to any one, is consequently understood to be improper for any other: or, at least, the same phraseology cannot belong to styles of an opposite character; and words of general use belong to no particular style.[238] For example: "So then it is not of him that *willeth*, nor of him that *runneth*, but of God that *showeth* mercy."—*Rom.*, ix, 16. If the termination *eth* is not obsolete, as some say it is, all verbs to which this ending is added, are of the solemn style; for the common or familiar expression would here be this; "So then it is not of him that *wills*, nor of him that *runs*, but of God that *shows* mercy." Ben Jonson, in his grammar, endeavoured to arrest this change of *eth* to *s*; and, according to Lindley Murray, (*Octavo Gram.*, p. 90,) Addison also injudiciously disapproved it.

In spite of all such objections, however, some future grammarian will probably have to say of the singular ending *eth*, as Lowth and Murray have already said of the plural *en*: "It was laid aside as unnecessary."

OBS. 10.—Of the origin of the personal terminations of English verbs, that eminent etymologist Dr. Alexander Murray, gives the following account: "The readers of our modern tongue may be reminded, that the terminations, *est, eth*, and *s*, in our verbs, as in *layest, layeth*, and *laid'st*, or *laidest*; are the faded *remains of the pronouns* which were formerly joined to the verb itself, and placed the language, in respect of concise expression, on a level with the Greek, Latin, and Sanscrit, its sister dialects."—*History of European Languages*, Vol. i, p. 52. According to this, since other signs of the persons and numbers are now employed with the verb, it is not strange that there should appear a tendency to lay aside such of these endings as are least agreeable and least necessary. Any change of this kind will of course occur first in the familiar style. For example: "Thou *wentest* in to men uncircumcised, and *didst eat* with them."—*Acts*, xi, 3. "These things write I unto thee, that thou *mayst* know how thou *oughtest* to behave thyself in the house of God."—*1 Tim.*, iii, 15. These forms, by universal consent, are now of the solemn style; and, consequently, are really good English in no other. For nobody, I suppose, will yet pretend that the inflection of our preterits and auxiliaries by *st* or *est*, is entirely *obsolete*;[239] and surely no person of any literary taste ever uses the foregoing forms familiarly. The termination *est*, however, has *in some instances* become obsolete; or has faded into *st* or *t*, even in the solemn style. Thus, (if indeed, such forms ever were in good use,) *diddest* has become *didst; havest, hast; haddest, hadst; shallest, shalt; willest, wilt*; and *cannest, canst. Mayest, mightest, couldest, wouldest*, and *shouldest*, are occasionally found in books not ancient; but *mayst, mightst, couldst, wouldst*, and *shouldst*, are abundantly more common, and all are peculiar to the solemn style. *Must, burst, durst, thrust, blest, curst, past, lost, list, crept, kept, girt, built, felt, dwelt, left, bereft*, and many other verbs of similar endings, are seldom, if ever, found encumbered with an additional *est*. For the rule which requires this ending, has always had many exceptions that have not been noticed by grammarians.[240] Thus Shakspeare wrote even in the present tense, "Do as thou *list*," and not "Do as thou *listest*." Possibly, however, *list* may here be reckoned of the subjunctive mood; but the following example from Byron is certainly in the indicative:—

"And thou, who never yet of human wrong *Lost* the unbalanced scale, great Nemesis!"—*Harold*, C. iv, st. 132.

OBS. 11.—Any phraseology that is really obsolete, is no longer fit to be imitated even in the solemn style; and what was never good English, is no more to be respected in that style, than in any other. Thus: "Art not thou that Egyptian, *which* before these days *madest* an uproar, and *leddest* out into the wilderness four thousand men that were murderers?"—*Acts*, xxi, 38. Here, (I think,) the version ought to be, "Art not thou that Egyptian, *who* a while ago *made* an uproar, and *led* out into the wilderness four thousand men, that were murderers?" If so, there is in this no occasion to make a difference between the solemn and the familiar style. But what is the familiar form of expression for the texts cited before? The fashionable will say, it is this: "*You went* in to men uncircumcised, and *did eat* with them."—"I write these things to *you*, that *you may know* how *you ought* to behave *yourself* in the house of God." But this is not *literally* of the singular number: it is no more singular, than *vos* in Latin, or *vous* in French, or *we* used for *I* in English, is singular. And if there remains to us any other form, that is both singular and grammatical, it is unquestionably the following: "*Thou went* in to men uncircumcised, and *did eat* with them."—"I write these things to *thee*, that thou *may know* how *thou ought* to behave *thyself* in the house of God." The acknowledged doctrine of all the teachers of English grammar, that the inflection of our auxiliaries and preterits by *st* or *est* is peculiar to "the solemn style," leaves us no other alternative, than either to grant the propriety of here dropping the suffix for the familiar style, or to rob our language of any familiar use of the pronoun *thou* forever. Who, then, are here the neologists, the innovators, the impairers of the language? And which is the greater *innovation*, merely to drop, on familiar occasions, or *when it suits our style*, one obsolescent verbal termination,—a termination often dropped *of old* as well as now,—or to strike from the conjugations of all our verbs one sixth part of their entire scheme?[241]

"O mother myn, that cleaped *were* Argyue,
Wo worth that day that thou me *bare* on lyue."—*Chaucer*.

OBS. 12.—The grammatical propriety of distinguishing from the solemn style both of the forms presented above, must be evident to every one who considers with candour the reasons, analogies, and authorities, for this distinction. The support of the latter is very far from resting solely on the practice of a particular sect; though this, if they would forbear to corrupt the pronoun while they simplify the verb, would deserve much more consideration than has ever been allowed it. Which of these modes of address is the more grammatical, it is useless to dispute; since fashion rules the one, and a scruple of conscience is sometimes alleged for the other. A candid critic will consequently allow all to take their choice. It is enough for him, if he can demonstrate to the candid inquirer, what phraseology is in any view allowable, and what is for any good reason reprehensible. That the use of the plural for the singular is ungrammatical, it is neither discreet nor available to affirm; yet, surely, it did not originate in any regard to grammar rules. Murray the schoolmaster, whose English Grammar appeared some years before that of Lindley Murray, speaks of it as follows: "*Thou*, the second person singular, though *strictly grammatical*, is seldom used, except in addresses to God, in poetry, and by the people called Quakers. In all other cases, a *fondness for foreign manners*,[242] and the power of custom, have given a sanction to the use of *you*, for the second person singular, though *contrary to grammar*,[243] and attended with this particular inconveniency, that a plural verb must be used to agree with the pronoun in number, and both applied to a *single person*; as, *you are*, or *you were*,—not *you wast*, or *you was*."—*Third Edition*, Lond., 1793, p. 34. This author everywhere exhibits the auxiliaries, *mayst, mightst, couldst, wouldst*, and *shouldst*, as words of one syllable; and also observes, in a marginal note, "Some writers begin to say, '*Thou may, thou might*,' &c."—*Ib.*, p. 36. Examples of this are not very uncommon: "Thou *shall* want ere I want."—*Old Motto; Scott's Lay*, Note 1st to Canto 3. "Thyself the mournful tale *shall* tell."—*Felton's Gram.*, p. 20.

"One sole condition would I dare suggest,
That *thou would save* me from my own request."—*Jane Taylor*.

OBS. 13.—In respect to the second person singular, the grammar of Lindley Murray makes no distinction between the solemn and the familiar style; recognizes in no way the fashionable substitution of *you* for *thou*; and, so far as I perceive, takes it for granted, that every one who pretends to speak or write grammatically, must always, in addressing an individual, employ the singular pronoun, and inflect the verb with *st* or *est*, except in the imperative mood and the subjunctive present. This is the more remarkable, because the author was a valued member of the Society of Friends; and doubtless his own daily practice contradicted his doctrine, as palpably as does that of every other member of the Society. And many a schoolmaster, taking that work for his text-book, or some other as faulty, is now doing precisely the same thing. But what a teacher is he, who dares not justify as a grammarian that which he constantly practices as a man! What a scholar is he, who can be led by a false criticism or a false custom, to condemn his own usage and that of every body else! What a casuist is he, who dares pretend conscience for practising that which he knows and acknowledges to be wrong! If to speak in the second person singular without inflecting our preterits and auxiliaries, is a censurable corruption of the language, the Friends have no alternative but to relinquish their scruple about the application of *you* to one person; for none but the adult and learned can ever speak after the manner of ancient books: children and common people can no more be brought to speak agreeably to any antiquated forms of the English language, than according to the imperishable models of Greek and Latin. He who traces the history of our vernacular tongue, will find it has either simplified or entirely dropped several of its ancient terminations; and that the *st* or *est* of the second person singular, *never was adopted* in any thing like the extent to which our modern grammarians have attempted to impose it. "Thus becoming unused to inflections, we lost the perception of their meaning and nature."— *Philological Museum*, i, 669. "You cannot make a whole people all at once talk in a different tongue from that which it has been used to talk in: you cannot force it to unlearn the words it has learnt from its fathers, in order to learn a set of newfangled words out of [a grammar or] a dictionary."—*Ib.*, i, 650. Nor can you, in this instance, restrain our poets from transgressing the doctrine of Lowth and Murray:—

"Come, thou pure Light,—which first in Eden *glowed*.
And *threw* thy splendor round man's calm abode."—*Alonzo Lewis*.

OBS. 14.—That which has passed away from familiar practice, may still be right in the solemn style, and may there remain till it becomes obsolete. But no obsolescent termination has ever yet been recalled into the popular service. This is as true in other languages as in our own: "In almost every word of the Greek," says a learned author, "we meet with contractions and abbreviations; but, I believe, the flexions of no language allow of extension or amplification. In our own we may write *sleeped* or *slept*, as the metre of a line or the rhythm of a period may require; but by no license may we write *sleepeed*."—*Knight, on the Greek Alphabet*, 4to, p. 107. But, if after contracting *sleeped* into *slept*, we add an *est* and make *sleptest*, is there not here an extension of the word from one syllable to two? Is there not an amplification that is at once novel, disagreeable, unauthorized, and unnecessary? Nay, even in the regular and established change, as of *loved* to *lovedst*, is there not a syllabic increase, which is unpleasant to the ear, and unsuited to familiar speech? Now, to what extent do these questions apply to the verbs in our language? Lindley Murray, it is presumed, had no conception of that extent; or of the weight of the objection which is implied in the second. With respect to a vast number of our most common verbs, he himself never knew, nor does the greatest grammarian now living know, in what way he ought to form the simple past tense in the second person singular, otherwise than by the mere uninflected preterit with the pronoun *thou*. Is *thou sleepedst* or *thou sleptest, thou leavedst* or *thou leftest, thou feeledst* or *thou feltest, thou dealedst* or *thou dealtest, thou tossedst* or *thou tostest, thou losedst* or *thou lostest, thou payedst* or *thou paidest, thou layedst* or *thou laidest*, better English than *thou slept, thou left, thou felt, thou dealt, thou tossed, thou lost, thou paid, thou laid?* And, if so, of the two forms in each instance, which is the right one? and why? The Bible has "*saidst*" and "*layedst*;" Dr. Alexander Murray, "*laid'st*" and "*laidest!*" Since the inflection of our preterits has never been orderly, and is now decaying and waxing old, shall we labour to recall what is so nearly ready to vanish away?

"Tremendous Sea! what time *thou lifted* up
Thy waves on high, and with thy winds and storms
Strange pastime *took*, and *shook* thy mighty sides
Indignantly, the pride of navies fell."—*Pollok*, B. vii, l. 611.

OBS. 15.—Whatever difficulty there is in ascertaining the true form of the preterit itself, not only remains, but is augmented, when *st* or *est* is to be added for the second person of it. For, since we use sometimes one and sometimes the other of these endings; (as, said_st_, saw_est_, bid_st_, knew_est_, loved_st_, went_est_;) there is yet need of some rule to show which we ought to prefer. The variable formation or orthography of verbs in the simple past tense, has always been one of the greatest difficulties that the learners of our language have had to encounter. At present, there is a strong tendency to terminate as many as we can of them in *ed*, which is the only regular ending. The pronunciation of this ending, however, is at least threefold; as in *remembered, repented, relinquished.* Here the added sounds are, first *d,* then *ed,* then *t*; and the effect of adding *st,* whenever the *ed* is sounded like *t,* will certainly be a perversion of what is established as the true pronunciation of the language. For the solemn and the familiar pronunciation of *ed* unquestionably differ. The present tendency to a regular orthography, ought rather to be encouraged than thwarted; but the preferring of *mixed* to *mixt, whipped* to *whipt, worked* to *wrought, kneeled* to *knelt,* and so forth, does not make *mixedst, whippedst, workedst, kneeledst,* and the like, any more fit for modern English, than are *mixtest, whiptest, wroughtest, kneltest, burntest, dweltest, heldest, giltest,* and many more of the like stamp. And what can be more absurd than for a grammarian to insist upon forming a great parcel of these strange and crabbed words for which he can quote no good authority? Nothing; except it be for a poet or a rhetorician to huddle together great parcels of consonants which no mortal man can utter,[244] (as *lov'dst, lurk'dst, shrugg'dst,*) and call them "*words.*" Example: "The clump of *subtonick* and *atonick* elements at the termination of *such words* as the following, is frequently, to the no small injury of articulation, particularly slighted: couldst, wouldst, hadst, prob'st, *prob'dst,* hurl'st, *hurl'dst,* arm'st, *arm'dst,* want'st, *want'dst,* burn'st, *burn'dst,* bark'st, *bark'dst,* bubbl'st, *bubbl'dst, troubbl'st, troubbl'dst.*"—*Kirkham's Elocution,*

p. 42. The word *trouble* may receive the additional sound of *st*, but this gentleman does not here *spell* so accurately as a great author should. Nor did they who penned the following lines, write here as poets should:—

"Of old thou *build'st* thy throne on righteousness."
—*Pollok's C. of T.*, B. vi, l. 638.

"For though thou *work'dst* my mother's ill."
—*Byron's Parasina*.

"Thou thyself *doat'dst* on womankind, admiring."
—*Milton's P. R.*, B. ii, l. 175.

"But he, the sev'nth from thee, whom thou *beheldst*."
—*Id., P. L.*, B. xi, l. 700.

"Shall build a wondrous ark, as thou *beheldst*."
—*Id., ib.*, B. xi, l. 819.

"Thou, who *inform'd'st* this clay with active fire!"
—*Savage's Poems*, p. 247.

"Thy valiantness was mine, thou *suck'dst* it from me."
—*Shak., Coriol.*, Act iii.

"This cloth thou *dipp'dst* in blood of my sweet boy."
—*Id., Henry VI*, P. i.

"Great Queen of arms, whose favour Tydeus won;
As thou *defend'st* the sire, defend the son."
—*Pope, Iliad*, B. x, l. 337.

OBS. 16.—Dr. Lowth, whose popular little Grammar was written in or about 1758, made no scruple to hem up both the poets and the Friends at once, by a criticism which I must needs consider more dogmatical than true; and which, from the suppression of what is least objectionable in it, has become, her hands, the source of still greater errors: "*Thou* in the polite, and even *in the familiar style, is disused,* and the plural *you* is employed instead of it; we say, *you have,* not *thou hast.* Though in this case, we apply *you* to a single person, yet the verb too *must agree with it in the plural number*; it must necessarily be, *you have,* not *you hast. You was* is an enormous solecism,[245] and yet authors of the first rank have inadvertently fallen into it. * * * On the contrary, the solemn style admits not of you for a single person. This *hath led* Mr. Pope into *a great impropriety* in the beginning of his Messiah:—

'O thou my voice inspire,
Who *touch'd* Isaiah's hallow'd lips with fire!'

The solemnity of the style would not admit of *you* for *thou,* in the pronoun; nor the measure of the verse *touchedst,* or *didst touch,* in the verb, as it *indispensably ought to be,* in the one or the other of those two forms; *you,* who *touched,* or *thou,* who *touchedst,* or *didst touch.*

'Just of *thy* word, in every thought sincere;
Who *knew* no wish, but what the world might hear.'—Pope.

It ought to be *your* in the first line, or *knewest* in the second. In order to avoid this *grammatical inconvenience*, the two distinct forms of *thou* and *you*, are often used promiscuously by our modern poets, in the same paragraph, and even in the same sentence, very inelegantly and improperly:—

'Now, now, I seize, I clasp *thy* charms;
And now *you burst*, ah cruel! from my arms.'—Pope."
  —*Lowth's English Gram.*, p. 34.

OBS. 17.—The points of Dr. Lowth's doctrine which are not sufficiently true, are the following: First, it is not true, that *thou*, in the familiar style, is *totally disused*, and the plural *you* employed universally in its stead; though Churchill, and others, besides the good bishop, seem to represent it so. It is now nearly two hundred years since the rise of the Society of Friends: and, whatever may have been the practice of others before or since, it is certain, that from their rise to the present day, there have been, at every point of time, many thousands who made no use of *you* for *thou*; and, but for the clumsy forms which most grammarians hold to be indispensable to verbs of the second person singular, the beautiful, distinctive, and poetical words, *thou, thyself, thy, thine*, and *thee*, would certainly be in no danger yet of becoming obsolete. Nor can they, indeed, at any rate, become so, till the fairest branches of the Christian Church shall wither; or, what should seem no gracious omen, her bishops and clergy learn to *pray in the plural number*, for fashion's sake. Secondly, it is not true, that, "*thou*, who touch'd," ought *indispensably* to be, "*thou*, who *touchedst*, or *didst touch*." It is far better to dispense with the inflection, in such a case, than either to impose it, or to resort to the plural pronoun. The "grammatical inconvenience" of dropping the *st* or *est* of a preterit, even in the solemn style, cannot be great, and may be altogether imaginary; that of imposing it, except in solemn prose, is not only real, but is often insuperable. It is not very agreeable, however, to see it added to some verbs, and dropped from others, in the same sentence: as,

"Thou, who *didst call* the Furies from the abyss,
And round Orestes *bade* them howl and hiss."
    —*Byron's Childe Harold*, Canto iv, st. 132.

"Thou *satt'st* from age to age insatiate,
And *drank* the blood of men, and *gorged* their flesh."
    —*Pollok's Course of Time*, B. vii, l. 700.

OBS. 18.—We see then, that, according to Dr. Lowth and others, *the only good English* in which one can address an individual on any ordinary occasion, is *you* with a plural verb; and that, according to Lindley Murray and others, *the only good English* for the same purpose, is *thou* with a verb inflected with *st* or *est*. Both parties to this pointed contradiction, are more or less in the wrong. The respect of the Friends for those systems of grammar which deny them the familiar use of the pronoun *thou*, is certainly not more remarkable, than the respect of the world for those which condemn the substitution of the plural *you*. Let grammar be a true record of existing facts, and all such contradictions must vanish. And, certainly, these great masters here contradict each other, in what every one who reads English, ought to know. They agree, however, in requiring, as indispensable to grammar, what is not only inconvenient, but absolutely impossible. For what "the measure of verse *will not admit*," cannot be used in poetry; and what may possibly be crowded into it, will often be far from ornamental. Yet our youth have been taught to spoil the versification of Pope and others, after the following manner: "Who *touch'd* Isaiah's hallow'd lips with fire." Say, "Who *touchedst* or *didst touch*."—*Murray's Key*, 8vo, p. 180. "For thee that ever *felt* another's wo." Say, "*Didst feel*."—*Ib*. "Who *knew* no wish but what the world might hear." Say, "Who *knewest* or *didst know*."—*Ib.* "Who all my sense *confin'd*." Say, "*Confinedst* or *didst confine*."—*Ib.*, p. 186. "Yet *gave* me in this dark estate." Say, "*Gavedst* or *didst give*."—*Ib.* "*Left* free the human will."—*Pope*. Murray's criticism extends not to this line, but by the analogy we must say, "*Leavedst* or *leftest*." Now it would be easier to fill a volume with such quotations, and such corrections, than to find sufficient authority to prove one such word as *gavedst, leavedst*, or *leftest*, to be really good English. If Lord Byron is authority for "*work'dst*," he is authority also for dropping the *st*, even where it might be added:—

    ——"Thou, who with thy frown
  *Annihilated* senates."
    —*Childe Harold's Pilgrimage*, Canto iv, st. 83.

OBS. 19.—According to Dr. Lowth, as well as Coar and some others, those preterits in which *ed* is sounded like *t*, "admit the change of *ed* into *t*; as, *snacht, checkt, snapt, mixt*, dropping also one of the double letters, *dwelt, past*."—*Lowth's Gram.*, p. 46. If this principle were generally adopted, the number of our regular verbs would be greatly diminished, and irregularities would be indefinitely increased. What confusion the practice must make in the language, especially when we come to inflect this part of the verb with *st* or *est*, has already been suggested. Yet an ingenious and learned writer, an able contributor to the Philological Museum, published at Cambridge, England, in 1832; tracing the history of this class of derivatives, and finding that after the *ed* was contracted in pronunciation, several eminent writers, as Spenser, Milton, and others, adopted in most instances a contracted form of orthography; has seriously endeavoured to bring us back to their practice. From these authors, he cites an abundance of such contractions as the following: 1. "Stowd, hewd, subdewd, joyd, cald, expeld, compeld, spoild, kild, seemd, benumbd, armd, redeemd, staind, shund, paynd, stird, appeard, perceivd, resolvd, obeyd, equald, foyld, hurld, ruind, joynd, scatterd, witherd," and others ending in *d*. 2. "Clapt, whipt, worshipt, lopt, stopt, stampt, pickt, knockt, linkt, puft, stuft, hist, kist, abasht, brusht, astonisht, vanquisht, confest, talkt, twicht," and many others ending in *t*. This scheme divides our regular verbs into three classes; leaving but very few of them to be written as they now are. It proceeds upon the principle of accommodating our orthography to the familiar, rather than to the solemn pronunciation of the language. "This," as Dr. Johnson observes, "is to measure by a shadow." It is, whatever show of learning or authority may support it, a pernicious innovation. The critic says, "I have not ventured to follow the example of Spenser and Milton throughout, but have merely attempted to revive the old form of the preterit in *t*."—*Phil. Museum*, Vol. i, p. 663. "We ought not however to stop here," he thinks; and suggests that it would be no small improvement, "to write *leveld* for *levelled, enameld* for *enamelled, reformd* for *reformed*," &c.

OBS. 20.—If the multiplication of irregular preterits, as above described, is a grammatical error of great magnitude; the forcing of our old and well-known irregular verbs into regular forms that are seldom if ever used, is an opposite error nearly as great. And, in either case, there is the same embarrassment respecting the formation of the second person. Thus *Cobbett*, in his English Grammar in a Series of Letters, has dogmatically given us a list of *seventy* verbs, which, he says, are, "by some persons, *erroneously deemed irregular*;" and has included in it the words, *blow, build, cast, cling, creep, freeze, draw, throw*, and the like, to the number of *sixty*; so that he is really right in no more than one seventh part of his catalogue. And, what is more strange, for several of the irregularities which he censures, his own authority may be quoted from the early editions of this very book: as, "For you could have *thrown* about seeds."—Edition of 1818, p. 13. "For you could have *throwed* about seeds."—Edition of 1832, p. 13. "A tree is *blown* down."—Ed. of 1818, p. 27. "A tree is *blowed* down."— Ed. of 1832, p. 25. "It *froze* hard last night. Now, what was it that *froze* so hard?"—Ed. of 1818, p. 38. "It *freezed* hard last night. Now, what was it that *freezed* so hard?"—Ed. of 1832, p. 35. A whole page of such contradictions may be quoted from this one grammarian, showing that *he did not know* what form of the preterit he ought to prefer. From such an instructor, who can find out what is good English, and what is not? Respecting the inflections of the verb, this author says, "There are three persons; *but, our verbs have no variation in their spelling, except for the third person singular.*"—*Cobbett's E. Gram.*, ¶ 88. Again: "Observe, however, that, in our language, there is no very great use in this distinction of modes; because, for the most part, our little *signs* do the business, and *they never vary in the letters of which they are composed.*"—*Ib.*, ¶ 95. One would suppose, from these remarks, that Cobbett meant to dismiss the pronoun *thou* entirely from his conjugations. Not so at all. In direct contradiction to himself, he proceeds to inflect the verb as follows: "I work, *Thou workest*, He works; &c. I worked, *Thou workedst*, He worked; &c. I shall or will work, *Thou shalt or wilt work*, He shall or will work;" &c.— *Ib.*, ¶ 98. All the *compound* tenses, except the future, he rejects, as things which "can only serve to fill up a book."

OBS. 21.—It is a common but erroneous opinion of our grammarians, that the unsyllabic suffix *st*, wherever found, is a modern contraction of the syllable *est*. No writer, however, thinks it always necessary to remind his readers of this, by inserting the sign of contraction; though English books are not a little disfigured by questionable apostrophes inserted for no other reason. Dr. Lowth says, "The nature of our language, the accent and pronunciation of it, inclines [incline] us to contract even all our regular verbs: thus *loved, turned*, are commonly pronounced in one syllable *lov'd, turn'd*: and the second person, which was originally in three syllables, *lovedest, turnedest*, is [say *has*] now become a dissyllable, *lovedst, turnedst*."—*Lowth's Gram.*, p. 45; *Hiley's*, 45; *Churchill's*, 104. See also *Priestley's Gram.*, p. 114; and *Coar's*, p. 102. This latter doctrine, with all its vouchers, still needs confirmation. What is it but an idle conjecture? If it were *true*, a few quotations might easily prove it; but when, and by whom, have any such words as *lovedest, turnedest,* ever been used? For aught I see, the simple *st* is as complete and as old a termination for the second person singular of an English verb, as *est*; indeed, it appears to be *older*: and, for the preterit, it is, and (I believe) *always has been*, the *most* regular, if not the *only* regular, addition. If *sufferedest, woundedest,* and *killedest,* are words more regular than *sufferedst, woundedst, killedst,* then are *heardest, knewest, slewest, sawest, rannest, metest, swammest,* and the like, more regular than *heardst, knewst, slewst, sawst, ranst, metst, swamst, satst, saidst, ledst, fledst, toldst,* and so forth; but not otherwise.[246] So, in the solemn style, we write *seemest, deemest, swimmest,* like *seemeth, deemeth, swimmeth,* and so forth; but, when we use the form which has no increase of syllables, why is an apostrophe more necessary in the second person, than in the third?—in *seemst, deemst, swimst,* than in *seems, deems, swims*? When final *e* is dropped from the verb, the case is different; as,

> "Thou *cutst* my head off with a golden axe,
> And *smil'st* upon the stroke that murders me."—*Shakspeare.*

OBS. 22.—Dr. Lowth supposes the verbal termination *s* or *es* to have come from a contraction of *eth*. He says, "Sometimes, by the rapidity of our pronunciation, the vowels are shortened or lost; and the consonants, which are thrown together, do not coalesce with one another, and are therefore changed into others of the same organ, or of a kindred species. This occasions a farther deviation from *the regular form*: thus, *loveth, turneth,* are contracted into *lov'th, turn'th,* and these, for easier pronunciation, *immediately* become *loves, turns.*"—*Lowth's Gram.*, p. 46; *Hiley's*, 45. This etymology may possibly be just, but certainly such contractions as are here spoken of, were not very common in Lowth's age, or even in that of Ben Jonson, who resisted the *s*. Nor is the sound of sharp *th* very obviously akin to flat *s*. The change would have been less violent, if *lov'st* and *turnst* had become *loves* and *turns*; as some people nowadays are apt to change them, though doubtless this is a grammatical error: as,

> "And wheresoe'er thou *casts* thy view."
> —*Cowley*.

> "Nor thou that *flings* me floundering from thy back."
> —*Bat. of Frogs and Mice*, 1,123.

> "Thou *sitt'st* on high, and *measures* destinies."
> —*Pollok, Course of Time*, B. vi, 1, 668.

OBS. 23.—Possibly, those personal terminations of the verb which do not form syllables, are mere contractions or relics of *est* and *eth*, which are syllables; but it is perhaps not quite so easy to prove them so, as some authors imagine. In the oldest specimens given by Dr. Johnson in his History of the English Language,—specimens bearing a much earlier date than the English language can claim,—even in what he calls "Saxon in its highest state of purity," both *st* and *th* are often added to verbs, without forming additional syllables, and without any sign of contraction. Nor were verbs of the second person singular always inflected of old, in those parts to which *est* was afterwards very commonly added. Examples: "Buton ic wat thæt thu *hoefst* thara wæpna."—*King Alfred*. "But I know that thou *hast* those weapons." "Thæt thu *oncnawe* thara worda sothfæstnesse. of tham the thu *geloered eart*."—*Lucæ*, i, 4. "That thou *mightest know* the certainty of those things wherein thou *hast been instructed*."—*Luke*, i, 4. "And thu *nemst* his naman Johannes."—*Lucæ*, i, 13. "And his name *schal be clepid* Jon."—*Wickliffe's Version*. "And thou *shalt call* his name John."—*Luke*, i, 13. "And he ne *drincth* win ne beor."—*Lucæ*, i, 15. "He *schal* not *drinke* wyn ne sydyr."—*Wickliffe*. "And *shall drink* neither wine nor strong drink."—*Luke*, i, 15. "And nu thu *bist* suwigende. and thu *sprecan* ne *miht* oth thone dæg the thas thing *gewurthath*. fortham thu minum wordum ne *gelyfdest*. tha *beoth* on hyra timan *gefyllede*."—*Lucæ*, i, 20. "And lo, thou *schalt* be doumbe, and thou *schalt* not mowe *speke*, til into the day in which these thingis *schulen be don*, for thou *hast* not *beleved* to my wordis, whiche *schulen be fulfild* in her tyme."—*Wickliffe*. "And, behold, thou *shalt* be dumb, and not able to speak, until the day *that*[247] these things *shall be performed*, because thou *believest* not my words, which *shall be fulfilled* in their season."—*Luke*, i, 20.

"In chaungyng of her course, the chaunge *shewth* this,
Vp *startth* a knaue, and downe there *falth* a knight."
—*Sir Thomas More*.

OBS. 24.—The corollary towards which the foregoing observations are directed, is this. As most of the peculiar terminations by which the second person singular is properly distinguished in the solemn style, are not only difficult of utterance, but are quaint and formal in conversation; the preterits and auxiliaries of our verbs are seldom varied in familiar discourse, and the present is generally simplified by contraction, or by the adding of *st* without increase of syllables. A distinction between the solemn and the familiar style has long been admitted, in the pronunciation of the termination *ed*, and in the ending of the verb in the third person singular; and it is evidently according to good taste and the best usage, to admit such a distinction in the second person singular. In the familiar use of the second person singular, the verb is usually varied only in the present tense of the indicative mood, and in the auxiliary *hast* of the perfect. This method of varying the verb renders the second person singular analogous to the third, and accords with the practice of the most intelligent of those who retain the common use of this distinctive and consistent mode of address. It disencumbers their familiar dialect of a multitude of harsh and useless terminations, which serve only, when uttered, to give an uncouth prominency to words not often emphatic; and, without impairing the strength or perspicuity of the language, increases its harmony, and reduces the form of the verb in the second person singular nearly to the same simplicity as in the other persons and numbers. It may serve also, in some instances, to justify the poets, in those abbreviations for which they have been so unreasonably censured by Lowth, Murray, and some other grammarians: as,

"And thou their natures *knowst*, and *gave* them names,
Needless to thee repeated."—*Milton*, P. L., Book vii, line 494.

OBS. 25.—The writings of the Friends, being mostly of a grave cast, afford but few examples of their customary manner of forming the verb in connexion with the pronoun *thou*, in familiar discourse. The following may serve to illustrate it: "Suitable to the office thou *layst* claim to."—R. BARCLAY'S *Works*, Vol. i, p. 27. "Notwithstanding thou *may have* sentiments opposite to mine."—THOMAS STORY. "To devote all thou *had* to his service;"—"If thou *should come*;"—"What thou *said*;"—"Thou kindly *contributed*;"—"The epistle which thou *sent* me;"—"Thou *would* perhaps *allow*;"—"If thou *submitted*;"—"Since thou *left*;"—"*Should* thou *act*;"—"Thou *may be* ready;"—"That thou *had met*;"—"That thou *had intimated*;"—"Before thou *puts*" [putst];—"What thou *meets*" [meetst];—"If thou *had made*;"—"I observed thou *was*;"—"That thou *might put* thy trust;"—"Thou *had been* at my house."—JOHN KENDALL. "Thou *may be plundered*;"—"That thou *may feel*;"—"Though thou *waited* long, and *sought* him;"—"I hope thou *will bear* my style;"—"Thou also *knows*" [knowst];—"Thou *grew* up;"—"I wish thou *would* yet *take* my counsel."— STEPHEN CRISP. "Thou *manifested* thy tender regard, *stretched* forth thy delivering hand, and *fed* and *sustained* us."—SAMUEL FOTHERGILL. The writer has met with thousands that used the second person singular in conversation, but never with any one that employed, on ordinary occasions, all the regular endings of the solemn style. The simplification of the second person singular, which, to a greater or less extent, is everywhere adopted by the Friends, and which is here defined and explained, removes from each verb eighteen of these peculiar terminations; and, (if the number of English verbs be, as stated by several grammarians, 8000,) disburdens their familiar dialect of 144,000 of these awkward and useless appendages.[248] This simplification is supported by usage as extensive as the familiar use of the pronoun *thou*; and is also in accordance with the canons of criticism: "The *first* canon on this subject is, All words and phrases which are remarkably harsh and unharmonious, and not absolutely necessary, should be rejected." See *Campbell's Philosophy of Rhetoric*, B. ii, Ch. ii, Sec. 2, Canon Sixth, p. 181. See also, in the same work, (B. hi, Ch. iv, Sec. 2d,) an *express defence* of "those elisions whereby the sound is improved;" especially of the suppression of the "feeble vowel in the last syllable of the preterits of our regular verbs;" and of "such abbreviations" as "the eagerness of conveying one's sentiments, the rapidity and ease of utterance, necessarily produce, in the dialect of conversation."—Pages 426 and 427. Lord Kames says, "That the English tongue, originally harsh, is at present much softened by dropping many *redundant consonants,* is undoubtedly true; that it is not capable of being further mellowed without suffering in its force and energy, will scarce be thought by any one who possesses an ear."—*Elements of Criticism*, Vol. ii, p. 12.

OBS. 26.—The following examples are from a letter of an African Prince, translated by Dr. Desaguillier of Cambridge, England, in 1743, and published in a London newspaper: "I lie there too upon the bed *thou presented* me;"—"After *thou* left me, in thy swimming house;"—"Those good things *thou presented* me;"—"When *thou spake* to the Great Spirit and his Son." If it is desirable that our language should retain this power of a simple literal version of what in others may be familiarly expressed by the second person singular, it is clear that our grammarians must not continue to dogmatize according to the letter of some authors hitherto popular. But not every popular grammar condemns such phraseology as the foregoing. "I improved, Thou *improvedst*, &c. This termination of the second person preterit, on account of its harshness, *is seldom used*, and especially in the irregular verbs."—*Harrison's Gram.*, p. 26. "The termination *est*, annexed to the preter tenses of verbs, is, at best, a very harsh one, when it is contracted, according to our general custom of throwing out the *e*; as *learnedst*, for *learnedest*; and especially, if it be again contracted into one syllable, *as it is commonly pronounced*, and made *learndst*. * * * I believe a writer or speaker would have recourse to any periphrasis rather than say *keptest*, or *keptst*. * * * Indeed this harsh termination *est* is *generally quite dropped in common conversation*, and sometimes by the poets, in writing."—*Priestley's Gram.*, p. 115. The fact is, it never was added with much uniformity. Examples: "But like the hell hounde *thou waxed* fall furious, expressing thy malice when *thou* to honour *stied*."—FABIAN'S CHRONICLE, V. ii, p. 522: in *Tooke's Divers.*, T. ii, p. 232.

> "Thou from the arctic regions came. Perhaps
> Thou noticed on thy way a little orb,
> Attended by one moon—her lamp by night."
>     —*Pollok*, B. ii, l. 5.

> "'So I believ'd.'—No, Abel! to thy grief,
> So thou *relinquish'd* all that was belief."
>     —*Crabbe, Borough*, p. 279.

OBS. 27.—L. Murray, and his numerous copyists, Ingersoll, Greenleaf, Kirkham, Fisk, Flint, Comly, Alger, and the rest; though they insist on it, that the *st* of the second person can never be dispensed with, except in the imperative mood and some parts of the subjunctive; are not altogether insensible of that monstrous harshness which their doctrine imposes upon the language. Some of them tell us to avoid this by preferring the auxiliaries *dost* and *didst*: as *dost burst*, for *burstest; didst check*, for *checkedst*. This recommendation proceeds on the supposition that *dost* and *didst* are smoother syllables than *est* and *edst*; which is not true: *didst learn* is harsher than either *learnedst* or *learntest*; and all three of them are intolerable in common discourse. Nor is the "*energy*, or *positiveness*," which grammarians ascribe to these auxiliaries, always appropriate. Except in a question, *dost* and *didst*, like *do, does*, and *did*, are usually signs of *emphasis*; and therefore unfit to be substituted for the *st, est*, or *edst*, of an unemphatic verb. Kirkham, who, as we have seen, graces his Elocution with such unutterable things, as "*prob'dst, hurl'dst, arm'dst, want'dst, burn'dst, bark'dst, bubbl'dst, troubbl'dst*," attributes the use of the plural for the singular, to a design of avoiding the raggedness of the latter. "In order to avoid the disagreeable harshness of sound, occasioned by the frequent recurrence of the termination *est, edst*, in the adaptation of our verbs to the nominative *thou*, a *modern innovation* which substitutes *you* for *thou*, in familiar style, has generally been adopted. This innovation contributes greatly to the harmony of our colloquial style. *You* was formerly restricted to the plural number; but now it is employed to represent either a singular or a plural noun."—*Kirkham's Gram.*, p. 99. A modern innovation, forsooth! Does not every body know it was current four hundred years ago, or more? Certainly, both *ye* and *you* were applied in this manner, to the great, as early as the fourteenth century. Chaucer sometimes used them so, and he died in 1400. Sir T. More uses them so, in a piece dated 1503.

"O dere cosyn, Dan Johan, she sayde,
What eyleth *you* so rathe to aryse?"—*Chaucer*.

Shakspeare most commonly uses *thou*, but he sometimes has *you* in stead of it. Thus, he makes Portia say to Brutus:

"*You* suddenly arose, and walk'd about, Musing, and sighing, with *your* arms across; And when I ask'd *you* what the matter was, *You* star'd upon me with ungentle looks."—*J. Cæsar*, Act ii, Sc. 2.

OBS. 28.—"There is a natural tendency in all languages to throw out the rugged parts which improper consonants produce, and to preserve those which are melodious and agreeable to the ear."—*Gardiner's Music of Nature*, p. 29. "The English tongue, so remarkable for its grammatical simplicity, is loaded with a great variety of dull unmeaning terminations. Mr. Sheridan attributes this defect, to an utter inattention to what is easy to the organs of speech and agreeable to the ear; and further adds, that, 'the French having been adopted as the language of the court, no notice was taken, of the spelling or pronunciation of our words, until the reign of queen Anne.' So little was spelling attended to in the time of Elizabeth, that Dr. Johnson informs us, that on referring to Shakspeare's will, to determine how his name was spelt, he was found to have written it himself [in] no *less* [fewer] than three different ways."—*Ib.*, p. 477. In old books, our participial or verbal termination *ed*, is found written in about a dozen different ways; as, *ed, de, d, t, id, it, yd, yt, ede, od, ud.* For *est* and *eth*, we find sometimes the consonants only; sometimes, *ist* or *yst, ith* or *yth*; sometimes, for the latter, *oth* or *ath*; and sometimes the ending was omitted altogether. In early times also the *th* was an ending for verbs of the third person plural, as well as for those of the third person singular;[249] and, in the imperative mood, it was applied to the second person, both singular and plural: as,

"*Demith* thyself, that demist other's dede; And trouthe the shall deliver, it's no drede."—*Chaucer*.

OBS. 29.—It must be obvious to every one who has much acquaintance with the history of our language, that this part of its grammar has always been quite as unsettled as it is now; and, however we may wish to establish its principles, it is idle to teach for absolute certainty that which every man's knowledge may confute. Let those who desire to see our forms of conjugation as sure as those of other tongues, study to exemplify in their own practice what tends to uniformity. The best that can be done by the author of a grammar, is, to exhibit usage, as it has been, and as it is; pointing out to the learner what is most fashionable, as well as what is most orderly and agreeable. If by these means the usage of writers and speakers cannot be fixed to what is fittest for their occasions, and therefore most grammatical, there is in grammar no remedy for their inaccuracies; as there is none for the blunders of dull opinionists, none for the absurdities of Ignorance stalled in the seats of Learning. Some grammarians say, that, whenever the preterit of an irregular verb is like the present, it should take *edst* for the second person singular. This rule, (which is adopted by Walker, in his Principles, No. 372,) gives us such words as *cast-edst, cost-edst, bid-dedst, burst-edst, cut-tedst, hit-tedst, let-tedst, put-tedst, hurt-edst, rid-dedst, shed-dedst,* &c. But the rule is groundless. The few examples which may be adduced from ancient writings, in support of this principle, are undoubtedly formed in the usual manner from regular preterits now obsolete; and if this were not the case, no person of taste could think of employing, on any occasion, derivatives so uncouth. Dr. Johnson has justly remarked, that "the chief defect of our language, is ruggedness and asperity." And this defect, as some of the foregoing remarks have shown, is peculiarly obvious, when even the regular termination of the second person singular is added to our preterits. Accordingly, we find numerous instances among the poets, both ancient and modern, in which that termination is omitted. See Percy's Reliques of Ancient Poetry, everywhere.

"Thou, who of old the prophet's eye *unsealed*."—*Pollok.*

"Thou *saw* the fields laid bare and waste."—*Burns.*[250]

OBS. 30.—With the familiar form of the second person singular, those who constantly put *you* for *thou* can have no concern; and many may think it unworthy of notice, because Murray has said nothing about it: others will hastily pronounce it bad English, because they have learned at school some scheme of the verb, which implies that this must needs be wrong. It is this partial learning which makes so much explanation here necessary. The formation of this part of speech, form it as you will, is *central to grammar*, and cannot but be very important. Our language can never entirely drop the pronoun *thou*, and its derivatives, *thy, thine, thee, thyself,* without great injury, especially to its poetry. Nor can the distinct syllabic utterance of the termination *ed* be now generally practised, except in solemn prose. It is therefore better, not to insist on those old verbal forms against which there are so many objections, than to exclude the pronoun of the second person singular from all such usage, whether familiar or poetical, as will not admit them. It is true that on most occasions *you* may be substituted for *thou*, without much inconvenience; and so may *we* be substituted for *I*, with just as much propriety; though Dr. Perley thinks the latter usage "is not to be encouraged."—*Gram.*, p. 28. Our authors and editors, like kings and emperors, are making *we* for *I* their most common mode of expression. They renounce their individuality to avoid egotism. And when all men shall have adopted this enallage, the fault indeed will be banished, or metamorphosed, but with it will go an other sixth part of every English conjugation. The pronouns in the following couplet are put for the first person singular, the second person singular, and the second person plural; yet nobody will understand them so, but by their antecedents:

"Right trusty, and so forth—*we* let *you* to know *We* are very ill used
by *you mortals* below."—*Swift.*

OBS. 31.—It is remarkable that some, who forbear to use the plural for the singular in the second person, adopt it without scruple, in the first. The figure is the same in both; and in both, sufficiently common. Neither practice is worthy to be made more general than it now is. If *thou* should not be totally sacrificed to what was once a vain compliment, neither should *I*, to what is now an occasional, and perhaps a vain assumption. Lindley Murray, who does not appear to have used *you* for *thou*, and who was sometimes singularly careful to periphrase [sic—KTH] and avoid the latter, nowhere in his grammar speaks of himself in the first person singular. He is often "the *Compiler*;" rarely, "the *Author*;" generally, "We:" as, "*We* have distributed these parts of grammar, in the mode which *we* think most correct and intelligible."—*Octavo Gram.*, p. 58. "*We* shall not pursue this subject any further."—*Ib.*, p. 62. "*We* shall close these remarks on the tenses."—*Ib.*, p. 76. "*We* presume no solid objection can be made."—*Ib.*, p. 78. "The observations which *we* have made."—*Ib.*, p. 100. "*We* shall produce a remarkable example of this beauty from Milton."—*Ib.*, p. 331. "*We* have now given sufficient openings into this subject."—*Ib.*, p. 334. This usage has authority enough; for it was not uncommon even among the old Latin grammarians; but he must be a slender scholar, who thinks the pronoun *we* thereby becomes *singular*. What advantage or fitness there is in thus putting *we* for *I*, the reader may judge. Dr. Blair did not hesitate to use *I*, as often as ho had occasion; neither did Lowth, or Johnson, or Walker, or Webster: as, "*I* shall produce a remarkable example of this beauty from Milton."—*Blair's Rhet.*, p. 129. "*I* have now given sufficient openings into this subject."—*Ib.*, p. 131. So in Lowth's Preface: "*I* believe,"—"*I* am persuaded,"—"*I* am sure,"—"*I* think,"—"*I* am afraid,"—"*I* will not take upon *me* to say."

OBS. 32.—Intending to be critical without hostility, and explicit without partiality, I write not for or against any sect, or any man; but to teach all who desire to know *the grammar* of our tongue. The student must distinctly understand, that it is necessary to speak and write differently, according to the different circumstances or occasions of writing. Who is he that will pretend that the solemn style of the Bible may be used in familiar discourse, without a mouthing affectation? In preaching, or in praying, the ancient terminations of *est* for the second person singular and *eth* for the third, as well as *ed* pronounced as a separate syllable for the preterit, are admitted to be generally in better taste than the smoother forms of the familiar style: because the latter, though now frequently heard in religious assemblies, are not so well suited to the dignity and gravity of a sermon or a prayer. In grave poetry also, especially when it treats of scriptural subjects, to which *you* put for *thou* is obviously unsuitable, the personal terminations of the verb, though from the earliest times to the present day they have usually been contracted and often omitted by the poets, ought still perhaps to be considered grammatically necessary, whenever they can be uttered, agreeably to the notion of our tuneless critics. The critical objection to their elision, however, can have no very firm foundation while it is admitted by some of the objectors themselves, that, "Writers *generally* have recourse to this mode of expression, that they may avoid harsh terminations."— *Irving's Elements of English Composition*, p. 12. But if writers of good authority, such as Pope, Byron, and Pollok, have sometimes had recourse to this method of simplifying the verb, even in compositions of a grave cast, the elision may, with tenfold stronger reason, be admitted in familiar writing or discourse, on the authority of general custom among those who choose to employ the pronoun *thou* in conversation.

"But thou, false Arcite, never *shall* obtain," &c.
—*Dryden, Fables.*

"These goods *thyself can* on thyself bestow."
—*Id., in Joh. Dict.*

"What I show, *thy self may* freely on thyself bestow."
—*Id., Lowth's Gram.*, p. 26.

"That thou *might* Fortune to thy side engage."
—*Prior*.

"Of all thou ever *conquered,* none was left."
—*Pollok*, B. vii, l. 760.

"And touch me trembling, as thou *touched* the man," &c.
—*Id.*, B. x, l. 60.

OBS. 33.—Some of the Friends (perhaps from an idea that it is less formal) misemploy *thee* for *thou*; and often join it to the third person of the verb in stead of the second. Such expressions as, *thee does, thee is, thee has, thee thinks,* &c., are double solecisms; they set all grammar at defiance. Again, many persons who are not ignorant of grammar, and who employ the pronoun aright, sometimes improperly sacrifice concord to a slight improvement in sound, and give to the verb the ending of the third person, for that of the second. Three or four instances of this, occur in the examples which have been already quoted. See also the following, and many more, in the works of the poet Burns; who says of himself, "Though it cost the schoolmaster some thrashings, I made an excellent English scholar; and, by the time I was ten or eleven years of age, I was a critic in substantives, VERBS, and particles:"—"But when thou *pours*;"—"There thou *shines* chief;"—"Thou *clears* the head;"—"Thou *strings* the nerves;"—"Thou *brightens* black despair;"—"Thou *comes*;"—"Thou *travels* far;"—"Now *thou's turned* out;"—"Unseen thou *lurks*;"—"O thou pale orb that silent *shines*." This mode of simplifying the verb, confounds the persons; and, as it has little advantage in sound, over the regular contracted form of the second person, it ought to be avoided. With this author it may be, perhaps, a Scotticism: as,

"Thou *paints* auld nature to the nines,
In thy sweet Caledonian lines."—*Burns to Ramsay*.

"Thou *paintst old* nature," would be about as smooth poetry, and certainly much better English. This confounding of the persons of the verb, however, is no modern peculiarity. It appears to be about as old as the use of *s* for *th* or *eth*. Spenser, the great English poet of the sixteenth century, may be cited in proof: as,

"Siker, *thou's* but a lazy loord,
And *rekes* much of thy swinke."—*Joh. Dict., w. Loord.*

OBS. 34.—In the solemn style, (except in poetry, which usually contracts these forms,) the second person singular of the present indicative, and that of the irregular preterits, commonly end in *est*, pronounced as a separate syllable, and requiring the duplication of the final consonant, according to Rule 3d for Spelling: as, I *run*, thou *runnest*; I *ran*, thou *rannest*. But as the termination *ed*, in solemn discourse, constitutes a syllable, the regular preterits form the second person singular by assuming *st*, without further increase of syllables: as, I *loved*, thou *lovedst*; not, "*lovedest*," as Chandler made it in his English Grammar, p. 41, Edition of 1821; and as Wells's rule, above cited, if literally taken, would make it. *Dost* and *hast*, and the three irregular preterits, *wast*, *didst*, and *hadst*, are permanently contracted; though *doest* and *diddest* are sometimes seen in old books. *Saidst* is more common, and perhaps more regular, than *saidest*. *Werest* has long been contracted into *wert*: "I would thou *werest* either cold or hot."—*W. Perkins,* 1608.[251] The auxiliaries *shall* and *will* change the final *l* to *t*, and become *shalt* and *wilt*. To the auxiliaries, *may, can, might, could, would*, and *should*, the termination *est* was formerly added; but they are now generally written with *st* only, and pronounced as monosyllables, even in solemn discourse. Murray, in quoting the Scriptures, very often charges *mayest* to *mayst*, *mightest* to *mightst*, &c. Some other permanent contractions are occasionally met with, in what many grammarians call the solemn style; as *bidst* for *biddest, fledst* for *fleddest, satst* for *sattest*:

"Riding sublime, thou *bidst* the world adore,
And humblest nature with thy northern blast."
　—*Thomson.*

"Fly thither whence thou *fledst*."
　—*Milton, P. L.*, B. iv, l. 963.

"Unspeakable, who *sitst* above these heavens."
—*Id., ib.*, B. v, l. 156.

"Why *satst* thou like an enemy in wait?"
—*Id., ib.*, B. iv, l. 825.

OBS. 35.—The formation of the third person singular of verbs, is *now* precisely the same as that of the plural number of nouns: as, *love, loves; show, shows; boast, boasts; fly, flies; reach, reaches.* This form began to be used about the beginning of the sixteenth century. The ending seems once to have been *es*, sounded as *s* or *z*: as,

"And thus I see among these pleasant thynges
Eche care *decayes*, and yet my sorrow *sprynges*."—*Earl of Surry.*

"With throte yrent, he *roares*, he *lyeth* along."—*Sir T. Wyat.*

"He *dyeth*, he is all dead, he *pantes*, he *restes*."—*Id.*, 1540.

In all these instances, the *e* before the *s* has become improper. The *es* does not here form a syllable; neither does the *eth*, in "*lyeth*" and "*dyeth*." In very ancient times, the third person singular appears to have been formed by adding *th* or *eth* nearly as we now add *s* or *es*[252] Afterwards, as in our common Bible, it was formed by adding *th* to verbs ending in *e*, and *eth* to all others; as, "For he that *eateth* and *drinketh* unworthily, *eateth* and *drinketh* damnation to himself."—*1 Cor.*, xi, 29. "He *quickeneth* man, who is dead in trespasses and sins; he *keepeth* alive the quickened soul, and *leadeth* it in the paths of life; he *scattereth, subdueth,* and *conquereth* the enemies of the soul."—*I. Penington.* This method of inflection, as now pronounced, always adds a syllable to the verb. It is entirely confined to the solemn style, and is little used. *Doth, hath,* and *saith,* appear to be permanent contractions of verbs thus formed. In the days of Shakspeare, both terminations were common, and he often mixed them, in a way which is not very proper now: as,

"The quality of mercy is not strained;
It *droppeth,* as the gentle rain from heaven
Upon the place beneath: it is twice bless'd;
It *blesseth* him that *gives,* and him that *takes.*"
    —*Merchant of Venice.*

OBS. 36.—When the second person singular is employed in familiar discourse, with any regard to correctness, it is usually formed in a manner strictly analogous to that which is now adopted in the third person singular. When the verb ends with a sound which will unite with that of *st* or *s,* the second person singular is formed by adding *s* only, and the third, by adding *s* only; and the number of syllables is not increased: as, I *read,* thou *readst,* he *reads;* I *know,* thou *knowst,* he *knows;* I *take,* thou *takest,* he *takes;* I *free,* thou *freest,* he *frees.* For, when the verb ends in mute *a,* no termination renders this *a* vocal in the familiar style, if a synæresis can take place. To prevent their readers from ignorantly assuming the pronunciation of the solemn style, the poets have generally marked such words with an apostrophe: as,

"Look what thy soul holds dear, imagine it
To lie the way thou *go'st,* not whence thou *com'st.*"—*Shak.*

OBS. 37.—But when the verb ends in a sound which will not unite with that of *st* or *s*, the second and third persons are formed by adding *est* and *es*; or, if the first person end in mute *e*, the *st* and *s* render that *e* vocal; so that the verb acquires an additional syllable: as, I *trace*, thou *tracest*, he *traces*; I *pass*, thou *passest*, he *passes*; I *fix*, thou *fixest*, he *fixes*; I *preach*, thou *preachest*, he *preaches*; I *blush*, thou *blushest*, he *blushes*; I *judge*, thou *judgest*, he *judges*. But verbs ending in *o* or *y* preceded by a consonant, do not exactly follow either of the foregoing rules. In these, *y* is changed into *i*; and, to both *o* and *i*, *est* and *es* are added without increase of syllables: as, I *go*, thou *goest*, he *goes*; I *undo*, thou *undoest*,[253] he *undoes*; I *fly*, thou *fliest*, he *flies*; I *pity*, thou *pitiest*, he *pities*. Thus, in the following lines, *goest* must be pronounced like *ghost*; otherwise, we spoil the measure of the verse:

"Thou *goest* not now with battle, and the voice
Of war, as once against the rebel hosts;
Thou *goest* a Judge, and *findst* the guilty bound;
Thou *goest* to prove, condemn, acquit, reward."—*Pollok*, B. x.

In solemn prose, however, the termination is here made a separate syllable: as, I *go*, thou *goëst*, he *goëth*; I *undo*, thou *undoëst*, he *undoëth*; I *fly*, thou *fliëst*, he *fliëth*; I *pity*, thou *pitiëst*, he *pitiëth*.

OBS. 38.—The auxiliaries *do, dost, does*,—(pronounced *doo, dust, duz*; and not as the words *dough, dosed, doze*,—) *am, art, is*,—*have, hast, has*,—being also in frequent use as principal verbs of the present tense, retain their peculiar forms, with distinction of person and number, when they help to form the compound tenses of other verbs. The other auxiliaries are not varied, or ought not to be varied, except in the solemn style. Example of the familiar use: "That thou *may* be found truly owning it."—*Barclay's Works*, Vol. i, p. 234.

OBS. 39.—The only regular terminations that are added to English verbs, are *ing, d* or *e, st* or *est, s* or *es, th* or *eth*[254] *Ing*, and *th* or *eth*, always add a syllable to the verb; except in *doth, hath, saith*.[255] The rest, whenever their sound will unite with that of the final syllable of the verb, are usually added without increasing the number of syllables; otherwise, they are separately pronounced. In solemn discourse, however, *ed* and *est* are by most speakers uttered distinctly in all cases; except sometimes when a vowel precedes: as in *sanctified, glorified*, which are pronounced as three syllables only. Yet, in spite of this analogy, many readers will have *sanctifiest* and *glorifiest* to be words of four syllables. If this pronunciation is proper, it is only so in solemn prose. The prosody of verse will show how many syllables the poets make: as,

"Thou *diedst*, a most rare boy, of melancholy!"
—*Shak., Cymb.*, Act iv, sc. 2.

"Had not a voice thus warn'd me: What thou *seest*,
What there thou *seest*, fair creature, is thyself."
—*Milton*, B. iv, l. 467.

"By those thou *wooedst* from death to endless life."
—*Pollok*, B. ix, l. 7.

"Attend: that thou art happy, owe to God;
That thou *continuest* such, owe to thyself"
—*Milton*, B. v, l. 520.

OBS. 40.—If the grave and full form of the second person singular must needs be supposed to end rather with the syllable *est* than with *st* only, it is certain that this form may be *contracted*, whenever the verb ends in a sound which will unite with that of *st*. The poets generally employ the briefer or contracted forms; but they seem not to have adopted a uniform and consistent method of writing them. Some usually insert the apostrophe, and, after a single vowel, double the final consonant before *st*; as, *hold'st, bidd'st, said'st, ledd'st, wedd'st, trimm'st, may'st, might'st,* and so forth: others, in numerous instances, add *st* only, and form permanent contractions; as, *holdst, bidst, saidst, ledst, wedst, trimst, mayst, mightst,* and so forth. Some retain the vowel *e,* in the termination of certain words, and suppress a preceding one; as, *quick'nest, happ'nest, scatt'rest, rend'rest, rend'redst, slumb'rest, slumb'redst*: others contract the termination of such words, and insert the apostrophe; as, *quicken'st, happen'st, scatter'st, render'st, render'dst, slumber'st, slumber'dst.* The nature and idiom of our language, "the accent and pronunciation of it," incline us to abbreviate or "contract even all our regular verbs;" so as to avoid, if possible, an increase of syllables in the inflection of them. Accordingly, several terminations which formerly constituted distinct syllables, have been either wholly dropped, or blended with the final syllables of the verbs to which they are added. Thus the plural termination *en* has become entirely obsolete; *th* or *eth* is no longer in common use; *ed* is contracted in pronunciation; the ancient *ys* or *is,* of the third person singular, is changed to *s* or *es,* and is usually added without increase of syllables; and *st* or *est* has, in part, adopted the analogy. So that the proper mode of forming these contractions of the second person singular, seems to be, to add *st* only; and to insert no apostrophe, unless a vowel is suppressed from the verb to which this termination is added: as, *thinkst, sayst, bidst, sitst, satst, lov'st, lov'dst, slumberst, slumber'dst.*

"And know, for that thou *slumberst* on the guard,
Thou shalt be made to answer at the bar."—*Cotton.*

OBS. 41.—Ho man deserves more praise for his attention to English pronunciation, than John Walker. His Pronouncing Dictionary was, for a long period, the best standard of orthoëpy, that our schools possessed. But he seems to me to have missed a figure, in preferring such words as *quick'nest, strength'nest,* to the smoother and more regular forms, *quickenst, strengthenst.* It is true that these are rough words, in any form you can give them; but let us remember, that needless apostrophes are as rough to the eye, as needless *st*'s to the ear. Our common grammarians are disposed to encumber the language with as many of both as they can find any excuse for, and vastly more than can be sustained by any good argument. In words that are well understood to be contracted in pronunciation, the apostrophe is now less frequently used than it was formerly. Walker says, "This contraction of the participial *ed*, and the verbal *en*, is so fixed an idiom of our pronunciation, that to alter it, would be to alter the sound of the whole language. It must, however, be regretted that it subjects our tongue to some of the most hissing, snapping, clashing, grinding sounds that ever grated the ears of a Vandal; thus, *rasped, scratched, wrenched, bridled, fangled, birchen, hardened, strengthened, quickened,* &c. almost frighten us when written as they are actually pronounced, as *rapt, scratcht, wrencht, bridl'd, fangl'd, birch'n, strength'n'd, quick'n'd,* &c.; they become still more formidable when used contractedly in the solemn style, which never ought to be the case; for here instead of *thou strength'n'st* or *strength'n'd'st, thou quick'n'st* or *quick'n'd'st,* we ought to pronounce *thou strength'nest* or *strength'nedst, thou quick'nest* or *quick'nedst,* which are sufficiently harsh of all conscience."—*Principles,* No. 359. Here are too many apostrophes; for it does not appear that such words as *strengthenedest* and *quickenedest* ever existed, except in the imagination of certain grammarians. In solemn prose one may write, *thou quickenest, thou strengthenest,* or *thou quickenedst, thou strengthenedst;* but, in the familiar style, or in poetry, it is better to write, *thou quickenst, thou strengthenst, thou quickened, thou strengthened.* This is language which it is possible to utter; and it is foolish to strangle ourselves with strings of rough consonants, merely because they are insisted on by some superficial grammarians. Is it not strange, is it not incredible, that the same hand should have written the two following lines, in the same sentence? Surely, the printer has been at fault.

> "With noiseless foot, thou *walkedst* the vales of earth"—
> "Most honourable thou *appeared*, and most
> To be desired."—*Pollok's Course of Time*, B. ix, l. 18, and l. 24.

OBS. 42.—It was once a very common practice, to retain the final *y*, in contractions of the preterit or of the second person of most verbs that end in *y*, and to add the consonant terminations *d*, *st*, and *dst*, with an apostrophe before each; as, *try'd* for *tried*, *reply'd* for *replied*, *try'st* for *triest*, *try'dst* for *triedst*. Thus Milton:—

> "Thou following *cry'dst* aloud, Return, fair Eve;
> Whom *fly'st* thou? whom thou *fly'st*, of him thou art."
> —*P. L.*, B. iv, l. 481.

This usage, though it may have been of some advantage as an index to the pronunciation of the words, is a palpable departure from the common rule for spelling such derivatives. That rule is, "The final *y* of a primitive word, when preceded by a consonant, is changed into *i* before an additional termination." The works of the British poets, except those of the present century, abound with contractions like the foregoing; but late authors, or their printers, have returned to the rule; and the former practice is wearing out and becoming obsolete. Of regular verbs that end in *ay*, *ey*, or *oy*, we have more than half a hundred; all of which usually retain the *y* in their derivatives, agreeably to an other of the rules for spelling. The preterits of these we form by adding *ed* without increase of syllables; as, *display, displayed; survey, surveyed; enjoy, enjoyed*. These also, in both tenses, may take *st* without increase of syllables; as, *display'st, display'dst; survey'st, survey'dst; enjoy'st, enjoy'dst*. All these forms, and such as these, are still commonly considered contractions, and therefore written with the apostrophe; but if the termination *st* is sufficient of itself to mark the second person singular, as it certainly is considered to be as regards one half of them, and as it certainly was in the Saxon tongue still more generally, then for the other half there is no need of the apostrophe, because nothing is omitted. *Est*, like *es*, is generally a syllabic termination; but *st*, like *s*, is not. As signs of the third person, the *s* and the *es* are always considered equivalent; and, as signs of the second person, the *st* and the *est* are sometimes, and ought to be always, considered so too. To all verbs that admit the sound, we add the *s* without marking it as a contraction for *es*; and there seems to be no reason at all against adding the *st* in like manner, whenever we choose to form the second person without adding a syllable to the verb. The foregoing observations I commend to the particular attention of all those who hope to write such English as shall do them honour—to every one who, from a spark of literary ambition, may say of himself,

———————-"I twine
My hopes of being remembered in my line
With my land's language."—*Byron's Childe Harold*, Canto iv, st. 9.


## THE CONJUGATION OF VERBS.

The conjugation of a verb is a regular arrangement of its moods, tenses, persons, numbers, and participles.

There are four PRINCIPAL PARTS in the conjugation of every simple and complete verb; namely, the *Present,* the *Preterit,* the *Imperfect Participle,* and the *Perfect Participle.*[256] A verb which wants any of these parts, is called *defective;* such are most of the auxiliaries.

An *auxiliary* is a short verb prefixed to one of the principal parts of an other verb, to express some particular mode and time of the being, action, or passion. The auxiliaries are *do, be, have, shall, will, may, can,* and *must,* with their variations.

## OBSERVATIONS.

OBS. 1.—The *present,* or the verb in the present tense, is radically the same in all the moods, and is the part from which all the rest are formed. The present infinitive is commonly considered *the root,* or *simplest form,* of the English verb. We usually place the *preposition* TO *before* it; but never when with an auxiliary it forms a compound tense that is not infinitive: there are also some other exceptions, which plainly show, that the word *to* is neither a part of the verb, as Cobbett, R. C. Smith, S. Kirkham, and Wells, say it is; nor a part of the infinitive mood, as Hart and many others will have it to be, but a distinct *preposition.* (See, in the *Syntax* of this work, Observations on Rule 18th.) The preterit and the perfect participle are regularly formed by adding *d* or *ed,* and the imperfect participle, by adding *ing,* to the present.

OBS. 2.—The moods and tenses, in English, are formed partly by inflections, or changes made in the verb itself, and partly by the combination of the verb or its participle, with a few short verbs, called *auxiliaries,* or *helping verbs.* This view of the subject, though disputed by some, is sustained by such a preponderance both of authority and of reason, that I shall not trouble the reader with any refutation of those who object to it. Murray the schoolmaster observes, "In the English language, the times and modes of verbs are expressed in a perfect, easy, and beautiful manner, by the aid of a few little words called *auxiliaries,* or *helping verbs.* The possibility of a thing is expressed by *can* or *could*; the liberty to do a thing, by *may* or *might*; the inclination of the will, by *will* or *would*; the necessity of a thing, by *must* or *ought, shall* or *should.* The preposition *to* is never expressed after the helping verbs, except after *ought.*"—*Alex. Murray's*

*Gram.*, p. 112. See nearly the same words in *Buchanan's English Syntax*, p. 36; and in *the British Gram.*, p. 125.

OBS. 3.—These authors are wrong in calling *ought* a helping verb, and so is Oliver B. Peirce, in calling "*ought to,*" and "*ought to have*" auxiliaries; for no auxiliary ever admits the preposition *to* after it or into it: and Murray of Holdgate is no less in fault, for calling *let* an auxiliary; because no mere auxiliary ever governs the objective case. The sentences, "He *ought* to *help* you," and, "*Let* him *help* you," severally involve two different moods: they are equivalent to, "It *is his duty* to *help* you;"—"*Permit* him *to help* you." Hence *ought* and *let* are not auxiliaries, but principal verbs.

OBS. 4.—Though most of the auxiliaries are defective, when compared with other verbs; yet these three, *do, be*, and *have*, being also principal verbs, are complete: but the participles of *do* and *have* are not used as auxiliaries; unless *having*, which helps to form the third or "compound perfect" participle, (as *having loved*,) may be considered such. The other auxiliaries have no participles.

OBS. 5.—English verbs are principally conjugated by means of auxiliaries; the only tenses which can be formed by the simple verb, being the present and the imperfect; as, I *love*, I *loved*. And even here an auxiliary is usually preferred in questions and negations; as, "*Do* you love?"—"You *do* not *love*." "*Did* he *love*?"—"He *did* not *love*." "*Do* I not yet *grieve*?"—"*Did* she not *die*?" All the other tenses, even in their simplest form, are compounds.

OBS. 6.—Dr. Johnson says, "*Do* is sometimes used superfluously, as *I* do *love*, *I* did *love*; simply for *I love*, or *I loved*; but this is considered as a *vitious* mode of speech."—*Gram., in 4to Dict.*, p. 8. He also somewhere tells us, that these auxiliaries "are not proper before *be* and *have*;" as, "*I do be,*" for *I am*; "*I did have*," for *I had*. The latter remark is generally true, and it ought to be remembered;[257] but, in the *imperative mood, be* and *have* will perhaps admit the emphatic word *do* before them, in a colloquial style: as, "Now *do be* careful;"—"*Do have* a little discretion." Sanborn repeatedly puts *do* before *be*, in this mood: as, "*Do* you *be. Do* you *be* guarded. *Do* thou *be. Do* thou *be* guarded."—*Analytical Gram.*, p. 150. "*Do* thou *be* watchful."—*Ib.*, p. 155. In these instances, he must have forgotten that he had elsewhere said positively, that, "*Do*, as an auxiliary, *is never used* with the verb *be* or *am*."—*Ib.*, p. 112. In the other moods, it is seldom, if ever, proper before *be*; but it is sometimes used before *have*, especially with a negative: as, "Those modes of charity which *do not have* in view the cultivation of moral excellence, are essentially defective."—*Wayland's Moral Science*, p. 428. "Surely, the law of God, whether natural or revealed, *does not have* respect merely to the external conduct of men."—*Stuart's Commentary on Romans*, p. 158. "And each day of our lives *do we have* occasion to see and lament it."—*Dr. Bartlett's Lecture on Health*, p. 5. "Verbs, in themselves considered, *do not have* person and number."—*R. C. Smith's New Gram.*, p. 21. [This notion of Smith's is absurd. Kirkham taught the same as regards "person."] In the following example, *does he* is used for *is*,—the auxiliary *is*,—and perhaps allowably: "It is certain from scripture, that the same person *does* in the course of life many times offend and *be* forgiven."—*West's Letters to a Young Lady*, p. 182.

OBS. 7.—In the compound tenses, there is never any variation of ending for the different persons and numbers, except in the *first auxiliary*: as, "Thou *wilt have finished* it;" not, "Thou *wilt hast finishedst* it;" for this is nonsense. And even for the former, it is better to say, in the familiar style, "Thou *will have finished* it;" for it is characteristic of many of the auxiliaries, that, unlike other verbs, they are not varied by *s* or *eth*, in the third person singular, and never by *st* or *est*, in the second person singular, except in the solemn style. Thus all the auxiliaries of the potential mood, as well as *shall* and *will* of the indicative, are without inflection in the third person singular, though *will*, as a principal verb, makes *wills* or *willeth*, as well as *willest*, in the indicative present. Hence there appears a tendency in the language, to confine the inflection of its verbs to *this tense only*; and to the auxiliary *have, hast, has*, which is essentially present, though used with a participle to form the perfect. *Do, dost, does*, and *am, art, is*, whether used as auxiliaries or as principal verbs, are always of the indicative present.

OBS. 8.—The word *need*,—(though, as a principal verb and transitive, it is unquestionably both regular and complete,—having all the requisite parts, *need, needed, needing, needed*,—and being necessarily inflected in the indicative present, as, I *need*, thou *needst* or *needest*, he *needs* or *needeth*,—) is so frequently used without inflection, when placed before an other verb to express a necessity of the being, action, or passion, that one may well question whether it has not become, under these circumstances, an *auxiliary* of the potential mood; and therefore proper to be used, like all the other auxiliaries of this mood, without change of termination. I have not yet knowingly used it so myself, nor does it appear to have been classed with the auxiliaries, by any of our grammarians, except Webster.[258] I shall therefore not presume to say now, with positiveness, that it deserves this rank; (though I incline to think it does;) but rather quote such instances as have occurred to me in reading, and leave the student to take his choice, whether to condemn as bad English the uninflected examples, or to justify them in this manner. "He that can swim, *need* not despair to fly."—*Johnson's Rasselas*, p. 29. "One therefore *needs* not expect to do it."—*Kirkham's Elocution*, p. 155. "In so doing I should only record some vain opinions of this age, which a future one *need* not know."—*Rush, on the Voice*, p. 345. "That a boy *needs* not be kept at school."—LISDSEY: *in Kirkham's Elocution*, p. 164. "No man *need* promise, unless he please."—*Wayland's Moral Science*, p. 312. "What better reason *needs* be given?"—*Campbell's Rhet.*, p. 51. "He *need* assign no other reason for his conduct."—*Wayland, ib.*, p. 214. "Sow there is nothing that a man *needs* be ashamed of in all this."—*Collier's Antoninus*, p. 45. "No notice *need* be taken of the advantages."—*Walker's Rhyming Dict.*, Vol. ii, p. 304. "Yet it *needs* not be repeated."—*Bicknell's Gram.*, Part ii, p. 51. "He *need* not be anxious."—*Greenleaf's Gram. Simplified*, p. 38. "He *needs* not be afraid."—*Fisk's Gram. Simplified*, p. 124. "He who will not learn to spell, *needs* not learn to write."—*Red Book*, p. 22. "The heeder *need* be under no fear."—*Greenleaf's Gram.*, p. 38.[259] "More *need* not be said about it."—*Cobbett's E. Gram.*, ¶ 272. "The object *needs* not be expressed."—*Booth's Introduct. to Dict.*, p. 37. "Indeed, there *need* be no such thing."—*Fosdick's De Sacy*, p. 71. "This *needs* to be illustrated."—*Ib.*, p. 81. "And no part of the sentence *need* be omitted."—*Parkhurst's Grammar for Beginners*, p. 114. "The learner *needs* to know what sort of words are called verbs."—*Ib.*, p. 6. "No one *need* be apprehensive of suffering by faults of this kind."—*Sheridan's Elocution*, p. 171. "The student who has bought any of the former copies *needs* not repent."—*Dr. Johnson, Adv. to Dict.* "He *need* not enumerate their names."—*Edward's First Lessons in Grammar*, p. 38. "A quotation consisting of a word or two only *need* not begin with a capital."—*Churchill's Gram.*, p. 383. "Their sex is commonly known, and *needs* not to be marked."—*Ib.*, p. 72; *Murray's Octavo Gram.*, 51. "One *need* only open Lord Clarendon's history, to find examples every where."—*Blair's Rhet.*, p. 108. "Their sex is commonly known, and *needs* not be marked."—*Lowth's Gram.*, p. 21; *Murray's Duodecimo Gram.*, p. 51. "Nobody *need* be afraid he shall not have scope enough."—LOCKE: *in Sanborn's Gram.*, p. 168. "No part of the science of language, *needs to be ever* uninteresting to the pursuer."—*Nutting's Gram.*, p. vii. "The exact amount of knowledge is not, and *need* not be, great."—*Todd's Student's Manual*, p. 44. "He *needs to* act under a motive which is all-pervading."—*Ib.*, p. 375. "What *need* be said, will not occupy a long space."—*Ib.*, p. 244. "The sign TO *needs* not always be used."—*Bucke's Gram.*, p. 96. "Such as he *need* not be ashamed of."—*Snelling's Gift for Scribblers*, p. 23.

"*Needst* thou—*need* any one on earth—despair?"—*Ib.*, p. 32.

"Take timely counsel; if your dire disease
Admits no cure, it *needs* not to displease."—*Ib.*, p. 14.

OBS. 9.—If *need* is to be recognized as an auxiliary of the potential mood, it must be understood to belong to two tenses; the present and the perfect; like *may, can*, and *must*: as, "He *need* not *go*, he *need* not *have gone*; Thou *need* not *go, Thou need* not *have gone*;" or, in the solemn style, "Thou *needst* not go, Thou *needst* not *have gone*." If, on the contrary, we will have it to be always a principal verb, the distinction of time should belong to itself, and also the distinction of person and number, in the parts which require it: as, "He *needs* not go. He *needed* not go; Thou *needst* not go, Thou *needed* not go;" or, in the solemn style, "Thou *needest* not go, Thou *neededst* not go." Whether it can be right to say, "He *needed* not *have gone*," is at least questionable. From the observations of Murray, upon relative tenses, under his thirteenth rule of syntax, it seems fair to infer that he would have judged this phraseology erroneous. Again, "He *needs* not *have gone*," appears to be yet more objectionable, though for the same reason. And if, "He *need* not *have gone*," is a correct expression, *need* is clearly proved to be an *auxiliary*, and the three words taken together must form the potential perfect. And so of the plural; for the argument is from the connexion of the tenses, and not merely from the tendency of auxiliaries to reject inflection: as, "They need not *have been* under great concern about their public affairs."—*Hutchinson's History*, i, 194, From these examples, it may be seen that an auxiliary and a principal verb have some essential difference; though these who dislike the doctrine of compound tenses, pretend not to discern any. Take some further citations; a few of which are erroneous in respect to time. And observe also that the regular verb sometimes admits the preposition *to* after it: "' There is great dignity in being waited for,' said one who had the habit of tardiness, and who *had* not much else of which he *need* be vain."—*Students Manual*, p. 64. "But he *needed* not *have gone* so far for more instances."— *Johnson's Gram. Com.*, p. 143. "He *need* not *have said*, 'perhaps the virtue.'"—*Sedgwick's Economy*, p. 196. "I *needed* not *to ask* how she felt."—*Abbott's Young Christian*, p. 84. "It *need* not *have been* so."—*Ib.*, p. 111. "The most unaccommodating politician *need* not absolutely *want* friends."—*Hunts Feast of the Poets*, p. iii. "Which therefore *needs* not be introduced with much precaution."—*Campbell's Rhet.*, p. 326. "When an obscurer term *needs* to be explained by one that is clearer."—*Ib.*, p. 367. "Though, if she had died younger, she *need* not *have known it*."—*West's Letters*, p. 120. "Nothing *need* be said, but that they were the *most perfect* barbarisms."—*Blair's Rhet.*, p. 470. "He *need* not go."—*Goodenow's Gram.*, p. 36. "He *needed* but use the word *body*."—LOCKE: *in Joh. Dict.* "He *need* not be required to use them."—*Parker's Eng. Composition*, p. 50. "The last consonant of *appear* need not be doubled."—*Dr. Webster*. "It *needs* the less *to be inforced*."—*Brown's Estimate*, ii, 158. "Of these pieces of his, we *shall not need to give* any particular account."—*Seneca's Morals*, p. vi "And therefore I *shall need say* the less of them."—*Scougal*, p. 1101. "This compounding of words *need* occasion no surprise."—*Cardell's Essay on Language*, p. 87.

"Therefore stay, thou *needst* not to be gone."—*Shakspeare.*

"Thou *need* na *start* awa sae hasty."—*Burns, Poems*, p. 15.

"Thou *need* na *jouk* behint the hallan."—*Id., ib.*, p. 67.

OBS. 10.—The auxiliaries, except *must,* which is invariable, have severally two forms in respect to tense, or time; and when inflected in the second and third persons singular, are usually varied in the following manner:—

**TO DO.**

**PRESENT TENSE; AND SIGN OF THE INDICATIVE PRESENT.**

*Sing.* I do, thou dost, he does; *Plur.* We do, you do, they do.

IMPERFECT TENSE; AND SIGN of THE INDICATIVE IMPERFECT.

*Sing.* I did, thou didst, he did; *Plur.* We did, you did, they did.

## TO BE.

**PRESENT TENSE; AND SIGN OF THE INDICATIVE PRESENT.**

*Sing.* I am, thou art, he is; *Plur.* We are, you are, they are.

**IMPERFECT TENSE; AND SIGN OF THE INDICATIVE IMPERFECT.**

*Sing.* I was, thou wast, he was; *Plur.* We were, you were; they were.

## TO HAVE.

**PRESENT TENSE; BUT SIGN OF THE INDICATIVE PERFECT.**

*Sing.* I have, thou hast, he has; *Plur.* We have, you have, they have.

**IMPERFECT TENSE; BUT SIGN OF THE INDICATIVE PLUPERFECT.**

*Sing.* I had, thou hadst, he had; *Plur.* We had, you had, they had.

## SHALL AND WILL.

These auxiliaries have distinct meanings, and, as signs of the future, they are interchanged thus:

**PRESENT TENSE; BUT SIGNS OF THE INDICATIVE FIRST-FUTURE.**

1. Simply to express a future action or event:—

*Sing.* I shall, thou wilt, he will; *Plur.* We shall, you will, they will.

2. To express a promise, command, or threat:—

*Sing.*: I will, thou shalt, he shall; *Plur.* We will, you shall, they shall.

**IMPERFECT TENSE; BUT, AS SIGNS, AORIST, OR INDEFINITE.**

1. Used with reference to duty or expediency:—

*Sing.* I should, thou shouldst, he should; *Plur.* We should, you should, they should.

2. Used with reference to volition or desire:—

*Sing.* I would, thou wouldst, he would; *Plur.* We would, you would, they would.

## MAY.

**PRESENT TENSE; AND SIGN OF THE POTENTIAL PRESENT.**

*Sing.* I may, thou mayst, he may; *Plur.* We may, you may, they may.

**IMPERFECT TENSE; AND SIGN OF THE POTENTIAL IMPERFECT.**

*Sing.* I might, thou mightst, he might; *Plur.* We might, you might, they might.

## CAN.

**PRESENT TENSE; AND SIGN OF THE POTENTIAL PRESENT.**

*Sing.* I can, thou canst, he can; *Plur.* We can, you can, they can.

**IMPERFECT TENSE; AND SIGN OF THE POTENTIAL IMPERFECT.**

*Sing.* I could, thou couldst, he could; *Plur.* We could, you could, they could.

## MUST.

**PRESENT TENSE; AND SIGN OF THE POTENTIAL PRESENT.**

*Sing.* I must, thou must, he must; *Plur.* We must, you must, they must.

If must is ever used in the sense of the Imperfect tense, or Preterit, the form is the same as that of the Present: this word is entirely invariable.

OBS. 11.—Several of the auxiliaries are occasionally used as mere expletives, being quite unnecessary to the sense: as, 1. DO and DID: "And it is night, wherein all the beasts of the forest *do* creep forth."—*Psalms*, civ, 20. "And ye, that on the sands with printless foot *do* chase the ebbing Neptune, and *do* fly him when he comes back."—*Shak.* "And if a man *did* need a poison now."—*Id.* This needless use of do and did is now avoided by good writers. 2. SHALL, SHOULD, and COULD: "'Men *shall* deal unadvisedly sometimes, which after-hours give leisure to repent of.' I *should* advise you to proceed. I *should* think it would succeed. He, it *should* seem, thinks otherwise."—*W. Allen's Gram.*, p. 65. "I *could* wish you to go."—*Ib.*, p. 71. 3. WILL, &c. The following are nearly of the same character, but not exactly: "The isle is full of noises; sometimes a thousand twanging instruments *will* hum about mine ears."—*Shak.* "In their evening sports she *would* steal in amongst them."—*Barbauld.*

"His listless length at noontide *would* he stretch."—*Gray.*

OBS. 12.—As our old writers often formed the infinitive in *en*, so they sometimes dropped the termination of the perfect participle. Hence we find, in the infancy of the language, *done* used for *do*, and *do* for *done*; and that by the same hand, with like changes in other verbs: as, "Thou canst nothing *done*."—*Chaucer.* "As he was wont to *done*."—*Id.* "The treson that to women hath be *do*."—*Id.* "For to *ben* honourable and free."—*Id.* "I am sworn to *holden* it secre."—*Id.* "Our nature God hath to him *unyte*."—*Douglas.* "None otherwise negligent than I you saie haue I not *bee*."—*Id.* See *W. Allen's E. Gram.*, p. 97.

"But netheless the thynge is *do*,
That fals god was soone *go*."—GOWER: *H. Tooke*, Vol. i, p. 376.

OBS. 13.—"*May* is from the Anglo-Saxon, *mægan,* to be able. In the parent language also, it is used as an auxiliary. It is exhibited by Fortescue, as a principal verb; 'They shall *may* do it:' i. e. they shall be able (to) do it."—*W. Allen's Gram.*, p. 70. "*May not,* was formerly used for *must not*; as, 'Graces for which we *may not* cease to sue.' Hooker."—*Ib.*, p. 91. "*May* frequently expresses doubt of the fact; as, 'I *may* have the book in my library, but I think I have not.' It is used also, to express doubt, or a consequence, with a future signification; as, 'I *may* recover the use of my limbs, but I see little probability of it.'—'That they *may* receive me into their houses.' *Luke*, xvi, 4."—*Churchill's Gram.*, p. 247. In these latter instances, the potential present is akin to the subjunctive. Hence Lowth and others improperly call "I *may love*," &c. the subjunctive mood. Others, for the same reason, and with as little propriety, deny that we have any subjunctive mood; alleging an ellipsis in every thing that bears that name: as, "'If it (*may*) *be* possible, live peaceably with all men.' Scriptures."—*W. Allen's Gram.*, p. 61. *May* is also a sign of wishing, and consequently occurs often in prayer: as, "*May* it be thy good pleasure;"—"O that it *may* please thee;"—"*Mayst* thou be pleased." Hence the potential is akin also to the imperative: the phrases, "Thy will be done,"—"*May* thy will be done,"—"Be thy will done,"—"*Let* thy will be done,"—are alike in meaning, but not in mood or construction.

OBS. 14.—*Can*, to be able, is etymologically the same as the regular verbs *ken*, to see, and *con*, to learn; all of them being derived from the Saxon *connan* or *cunnan*, to know: whence also the adjective cunning, which was formerly a participle. In the following example *will* and *can* are principal verbs: "In evil, the best condition is, not to *will*; the second, not to *can*."—*Ld. Bacon.* "That a verb which signifies knowledge, may also signify power, appears from these examples: *Je ne saurois, I should not know how*, (i. e. *could* not.) [Greek: Asphalisasthe hos oidate], Strengthen it as you *know how*, (i. e. as you *can*.) *Nescio* mentiri, I *know not how to* (i.e. *I cannot*) lie."—*W. Allen's Gram.*, p. 71. *Shall*, Saxon *sceal*, originally signified to *owe*; for which reason *should* literally means *ought*. In the following example from Chaucer, *shall* is a principal verb, with its original meaning:

"For, by the faith I *shall* to God, I wene,
Was neuer straungir none in hir degre."—*W. Allen's Gram.*, p. 64.

OBS. 15.—*Do* and *did* are auxiliary only to the present infinitive, or the radical verb; as, *do throw, did throw*: thus the mood of *do throw* or *to throw* is marked by *do* or *to*. *Be*, in all its parts, is auxiliary to either of the simple participles; as, *to be throwing, to be thrown; I am throwing, I am thrown*: and so, through the whole conjugation. *Have* and *had*, in their literal use, are auxiliary to the perfect participle only; as, *have thrown, had thrown. Have* is from the Saxon *habban*, to possess; and, from the nature of the perfect participle, the tenses thus formed, suggest in general a completion of the action. The French idiom is similar to this: as, *J'ai vu*, I have seen. *Shall* and *should, will* and *would, may* and *might, can* and *could, must*, and also *need, (if we call the last a helping verb,) are severally auxiliary to both forms of the infinitive, and to these only: as, shall throw, shall have thrown; should throw, should have thrown*; and so of all the rest.

OBS. 16.—The form of the indicative pluperfect is sometimes used in lieu of the potential pluperfect; as, "If all the world could have seen it, the wo *had been* universal."—*Shakspeare*. That is,—"*would have been* universal." "I *had been drowned*, but that the shore was shelvy and shallow."—*Id*. That is,—"I *should have been drowned*." This mode of expression may be referred to the figure *enallage*, in which one word or one modification is used for an other. Similar to this is the use of *were* for *would be*: "It *were* injustice to deny the execution of the law to any individual;" that is, "it *would* be injustice."—*Murray's Grammar*, p. 89. In some instances, *were* and *had been* seem to have the same import; as, "Good *were* it for that man if he had never been born."—*Mark*, xiv, 21. "It *had been* good for that man if he had not been born."—*Matt.*, xxvi, 24. In prose, all these licenses are needless, if not absolutely improper. In poetry, their brevity may commend them to preference; but to this style, I think, they ought to be confined: as,

"That *had been* just, replied the reverend bard;
But done, fair youth, thou ne'er *hadst met* me here."—*Pollok.*

"The keystones of the arch!—though all were o'er,
For us repeopled *were* the solitary shore."—*Byron.*

OBS. 17.—With an adverb of comparison or preference, as *better, rather, best, as lief,* or *as lieve,* the auxiliary *had* seems sometimes to be used before the infinitive to form the potential imperfect or pluperfect: as, "He that loses by getting, *had better lose* than get."—*Penn's Maxims.* "Other prepositions *had better have been substituted.*"— *Priestley's Gram.,* p. 166. "I had as lief say."—LOWTH: *ib.,* p. 110. "It compels me to think of that which I *had rather forget.*"— *Bickersteth, on Prayer,* p. 25. "You *had much better say* nothing upon the subject."—*Webster's Essays,* p. 147. "I *had much rather show* thee what hopes thou hast before thee."—*Baxter.* "I *had rather speak* five words with my understanding, than ten thousand words in an unknown tongue."—*1 Cor.,* xiv, 19. "I knew a gentleman in America who told me *how much rather he had be* a woman than the man he is."— *Martineau's Society in America,* Vol. i, p. 153. "I *had as lief go* as not."— *Webster's Dict., w. Lief.* "I *had as lieve* the town crier spoke my lines."— SHAK.: *Hamlet.* "We *had best leave* nature to her own operations."— *Kames, El. of Crit.,* Vol. i, p. 310. "What method *had he best take*?"— *Harris's Hermes,* p. ix. These are equivalent to the phrases, *might better lose—might* better have been substituted—*would* as lief say—*would* rather forget—*might* much better say—*would* much rather show—*would* rather speak—how much rather he *would* be—*would* as lief go—*should* best leave —*might* he best take; and, for the sake of regularity, these latter forms ought to be preferred, as they sometimes are: thus, "For my own part, I *would rather look* upon a tree in all its luxuriancy."—*Addison, Spect.,* No. 414; *Blair's Rhet.,* p. 223. The following construction is different: "Augustus *had like to* have been slain."—*S. Butler.* Here *had* is a principal verb of the indicative imperfect. The following examples appear to be positively erroneous: "Much that was said, *had better remained* unsaid."—*N. Y. Observer*. Say, "*might better have remained*." "A man that is lifting a weight, if he put not sufficient strength to it, *had as good* put none at all."—*Baxter*. Say, "*might as well put*." "You *were better pour* off the first infusion, and use the latter."—*Bacon*. Say, "*might better pour;*" or, if you prefer it, "*had better pour.*" Shakspeare has an expression which is still worse:—

"Or, by the worth of mine eternal soul,
Thou *hadst been better have been born* a dog."—*Beauties*, p. 295.

OBS. 18.—The form of conjugating the active verb, is often called the *Active Voice*, and that of the passive verb, the *Passive Voice*. These terms are borrowed from the Latin and Greek grammars, and, except as serving to diversify expression, are of little or no use in English grammar. Some grammarians deny that there is any propriety in them, with respect to any language. De Sacy, after showing that the import of the verb does not always follow its form of voice, adds: "We must, therefore, carefully distinguish the Voice of a Verb from its signification. To facilitate the distinction, I denominate that an *Active* Verb which contains an Attribute in which the action is considered as performed by the Subject; and that a *Passive* Verb which contains an Attribute in which the action is considered as suffered by the Subject, and performed upon it by some agent. I call that voice a *Subjective* Voice which is generally appropriated to the Active Verb, and that an *Objective* Voice which is generally appropriated to the Passive Verb. As to the Neuter Verbs, if they possess a peculiar form, I call it a Neuter Voice."—*Fosdick's Translation*, p. 99.

OBS. 19.—A recognition of the difference between actives and passives, in our original classification of verbs with respect to their signification,— a principle of division very properly adopted in a great majority of our grammars and dictionaries, but opinionately rejected by Webster, Bolles, and sundry late grammarians,—renders it unnecessary, if not improper, to place Voices, the Active Voice and the Passive, among the *modifications* of our verbs, or to speak of them as such in the conjugations. So must it be in respect to "a Neuter Voice," or any other distinction which the classification involves. The significant characteristic is not overlooked; the distinction is not neglected as nonessential; but it is transferred to a different category. Hence I cannot exactly approve of the following remark, which "the Rev. W. Allen" appears to cite with approbation: "'The distinction of active or passive,' says the accurate Mr. Jones, '*is not essential* to verbs. In the infancy of language, it was, in all probability, not known. In Hebrew, the difference but imperfectly exists, and, in the early periods of it, probably did not exist at all. In Arabic, the only distinction which obtains, arises from the vowel points, a late invention compared with the antiquity of that language. And in our own tongue, the names of *active* and *passive* would have remained unknown, if they had not been learnt in Latin.'"—*Allen's Elements of English Gram.*, p. 96.

OBS. 20.—By *the conjugation* of a verb, some teachers choose to understand nothing more than the naming of its principal parts; giving to the arrangement of its numbers and persons, through all the moods and tenses, the name of *declension.* This is a misapplication of terms, and the distinction is as needless, as it is contrary to general usage. Dr. Bullions, long silent concerning principal parts, seems now to make a singular distinction between "*conjugating*" and "*conjugation.*" His *conjugations* include the moods, tenses, and inflections of verbs; but he teaches also, with some inaccuracy, as follows: "The principal parts of the verb are the *Present indicative,* the *Past indicative* and the *Past participle.* The mentioning of these parts is called CONJUGATING THE VERB."—*Analyt. and Pract. Gram.*, 1849, p. 80.

OBS. 21.—English verbs having but very few inflections to indicate to what part of the scheme of moods and tenses they pertain, it is found convenient to insert in our conjugations the preposition *to,* to mark the infinitive; personal *pronouns,* to distinguish the persons and numbers; the conjunction *if,* to denote the subjunctive mood; and the adverb *not,* to show the form of negation. With these additions, or indexes, a verb may be conjugated in *four ways*:—

1. Affirmatively; as, I write, I do write, or, I am writing; and so on.

2. Negatively; as, I write not, I do not write, or, I am not writing.

3. Interrogatively; as, Write I? Do I write? or, Am I writing?

4. Interrogatively and negatively; as, Write I not? Do I not write? or, Am I not writing?

**1. SIMPLE FORM, ACTIVE OR NEUTER.**

The simplest form of an English conjugation, is that which makes the present and imperfect tenses without auxiliaries; but, even in these, auxiliaries are required for the potential mood, and are often preferred for the indicative.

**FIRST EXAMPLE.**

*The regular active verb LOVE, conjugated affirmatively.*

**PRINCIPAL PARTS.**

*Present. Preterit. Imperfect Participle. Perfect Participle.* Love. Loved. Loving. Loved.

# INFINITIVE MOOD.[260]

The infinitive mood is that form of the verb, which expresses the being, action, or passion, in an unlimited manner, and without person or number. It is used only in the present and perfect tenses.

**PRESENT TENSE.**

This tense is the *root*, or *radical verb*; and is usually preceded by the preposition *to*, which shows its relation to some other word: thus,

To love.

**PERFECT TENSE.**

This tense prefixes the auxiliary *have* to the perfect participle; and, like the infinitive present, is usually preceded by the preposition *to*: thus,

To have loved.

**INDICATIVE MOOD.**

The indicative mood is that form of the verb, which simply indicates or declares a thing, or asks a question. It is used in all the tenses.

**PRESENT TENSE.**

The present indicative, in its simple form, is essentially the same as the present infinitive, or radical verb; except that the verb *be* has *am* in the indicative.

1. The simple form of the present tense is varied thus:—

*Singular. Plural.* 1st person, I love, 1st person. We love, 2d person, Thou lovest, 2d person, You love, 3d person, He loves; 3d person, They love.

2. This tense may also be formed by prefixing the auxiliary *do* to the verb: thus,

*Singular. Plural.* 1. I do love, 1. We do love, 2. Thou dost love, 2. You do love, 3. He does love; 3. They do love.

**IMPERFECT TENSE.**

This tense, in its simple form is *the preterit*; which, in all regular verbs, adds *d* or *ed* to the present, but in others is formed variously.

1. The simple form of the imperfect tense is varied thus:—

*Singular. Plural.* 1. I loved, 1. We loved, 2. Thou lovedst, 2. You loved, 3. He loved; 3. They loved.

2. This tense may also be formed by prefixing the auxiliary *did* to the present: thus,

*Singular. Plural.* 1. I did love, 1. We did love, 2. Thou didst love, 2. You did love, 3. He did love; 3. They did love.

**PERFECT TENSE.**

This tense prefixes the auxiliary *have* to the perfect participle: thus,

*Singular. Plural.* 1. I have loved, 1. We have loved, 2. Thou hast loved, 2. You have loved, 3. He has loved; 3. They have loved.

**IMPERFECT TENSE.**

This tense prefixes the auxiliary *had* to the perfect participle: thus,

*Singular. Plural.* 1. I had loved, 1. We had loved, 2. Thou hadst loved, 2. You had loved, 3. He had loved; 3. They had loved.

**FIRST-FUTURE TENSE.**

This tense prefixes the auxiliary *shall* or *will* to the present: thus,

1. Simply to express a future action or event:—

*Singular. Plural.* 1. I shall love, 1. We shall love, 2. Thou wilt love, 2. You will love, 3. He will love; 3. They will love;

2. To express a promise, volition, command, or threat:—

*Singular. Plural.* 1. I will love, 1. We will love, 2. Thou shalt love, 2. You shall love, 3. He shall love; 3. They shall love.

**SECOND-FUTURE TENSE.**

This tense prefixes the auxiliaries *shall have* or *will have* to the perfect participle: thus,

*Singular. Plural.* 1. I shall have loved, 1. We shall have loved, 2. Thou wilt have loved, 2. You will have loved, 3. He will have loved; 3. They will have loved.

OBS.—The auxiliary *shall* may also be used in the second and third persons of this tense, when preceded by a conjunction expressing condition or contingency; as, "*If* he *shall have completed* the work by midsummer."—*L. Murray's Gram.*, p. 80. So, with the conjunctive adverb *when*; as, "Then cometh the end, *when* he *shall have delivered* up the kingdom to God, even the Father; *when* he *shall have put* down all rule and all authority and power."—*1 Cor.*, xv, 24. And perhaps *will* may here be used in the first person to express a promise, though such usage, I think, seldom occurs. Professor Fowler has given to this tense, first, the "*Predictive*" form, as exhibited above, and then a form which he calls "*Promissive,*" and in which the auxiliaries are varied thus: "Singular. 1. I *will* have taken. 2. Thou *shalt* have taken, you *shall* have taken. 3. He *shall* have taken. Plural. 1. We *will* have taken. 2. Ye *or* you *shall* have taken. 3. He [say *They,*] *shall* have taken."—*Fowler's E. Gram.*, 8vo., N. Y., 1850, p. 281. But the other instances just cited show that such a form is not always promissory.

## POTENTIAL MOOD.

The potential mood is that form of the verb, which expresses the power, liberty, possibility, or necessity of the being, action, or passion. It is used in the first four tenses; but the potential *imperfect* is properly an *aorist*: its time is very indeterminate; as, "He *would be* devoid of sensibility were he not greatly satisfied."—*Lord Kames, El. of Crit.*, Vol. i, p. 11.

## PRESENT TENSE.

This tense prefixes the auxiliary *may, can,* or *must,* to the radical verb: thus,

*Singular*. *Plural.* 1. I may love, 1. We may love, 2. Thou mayst love, 2. You may love, 3. He may love; 3. They may love.

## IMPERFECT TENSE.

This tense prefixes the auxiliary *might, could, would,* or *should,* to the radical verb: thus,

*Singular. Plural.* 1. I might love, 1. We might love, 2. Thou mightst love, 2. You might love, 3. He might love; 3. They might love.

## PERFECT TENSE.

This tense prefixes the auxiliaries, *may have, can have,* or *must have,* to the perfect participle: thus,

*Singular. Plural.* 1. I may have loved, 1. We may have loved, 2. Thou mayst have loved, 2. You may have loved, 3. He may have loved; 3. They may have loved.

## PLUPERFECT TENSE.

This tense prefixes the auxiliaries, *might have, could have, would have,* or *should have,* to the perfect participle: thus,

*Singular. Plural.* 1. I might have loved, 1. We might have loved, 2. Thou mightst have loved, 2. You might have loved, 3. He might have loved; 3. They might have loved.

## SUBJUNCTIVE MOOD.

The subjunctive mood is that form of the verb, which represents the being, action, or passion, as conditional, doubtful, or contingent. This mood is generally preceded by a conjunction; as, *if, that, though, lest, unless, except.* But sometimes, especially in poetry, it is formed by a mere placing of the verb before the nominative; as, "*Were I,*" for, "*If I were;*"—"*Had he,*" for, "*If he had;*"—"*Fall we*" for, "*If we fall;*"—"*Knew they,*" for, "*If they knew.*" It does not vary its termination at all, in the different persons.[261] It is used in the present, and sometimes in the imperfect tense; rarely—and perhaps never *properly*—in any other. As this mood can be used only in a dependent clause, the *time* implied in its tenses is always relative, and generally indefinite; as,

"It shall be in eternal restless change,
Self-fed, and self-consum'd: *if this fail*,
The pillar'd firmament is rottenness."—*Milton, Comus*, l. 596.

**PRESENT TENSE.**

This tense is generally used to express some condition on which a future action or event is affirmed. It is therefore erroneously considered by some grammarians, as an elliptical form of the future.

*Singular. Plural.* 1. If I love, 1. If we love, 2. If Thou love, 2. If you love, 3. If He love; 3. If they love.

OBS.—In this tense, the auxiliary *do* is sometimes employed; as, "If thou *do prosper* my way."—*Genesis*, xxiv, 42. "If he *do* not *utter* it."—*Leviticus*, v, 1. "If he *do* but *intimate* his desire."—*Murray's Key*, p. 207. "If he *do promise*, he will certainly perform."—*Ib.*, p. 208. "An event which, if it ever *do occur*, must occur in some future period."—*Hiley's Gram.*, (3d Ed., Lond.,) p. 89. "If he *do* but *promise*, thou art safe."—*Ib.*, 89.

"Till old experience *do attain*
To something like prophetic strain."—MILTON: *Il Penseroso*.

These examples, if they are right, prove the tense to be *present*, and not *future*, as Hiley and some others suppose it to be.

**IMPERFECT TENSE.**

This tense, like the imperfect of the potential mood, with which it is frequently connected, is properly an aorist, or indefinite tense; for it may refer to time past, present, or future: as, "If therefore perfection *were* by the Levitical priesthood, what further need *was* there that an other priest *should rise*?"—*Heb.*, vii, 11. "They must be viewed *exactly* in the same light, as if the intention to purchase *now existed*."—*Murray's Parsing Exercises*, p. 24. "If it *were* possible, they *shall deceive* the very elect."—*Matt.*, xxiv, 24. "If the whole body *were* an eye, where *were* the hearing?"—*1 Corinthians*, xii, 17. "If the thankful *refrained*, it *would be* pain and grief to them."—*Atterbury*.

*Singular. Plural.* 1. If I loved, 1. If we loved, 2. If thou loved, 2. If you loved, 3. If he loved; 3. If they loved.

OBS.—In this tense, the auxiliary *did* is sometimes employed. The subjunctive may here be distinguished from the indicative, by these circumstances; namely, that the time is indefinite, and that the supposition is always contrary to the fact: as, "Great is the number of those who might attain to true wisdom, if they *did not already think* themselves wise."—*Dillwyn's Reflections*, p. 36. This implies that they *do think* themselves wise; but an indicative supposition or concession—(as, "Though they *did not think* themselves wise, they were so—") accords with the fact, and with the literal time of the tense,—here time past. The subjunctive imperfect, suggesting the idea of what is not, and known by the sense, is sometimes introduced without any of the *usual signs*; as, "In a society of perfect men, *where all understood* what was morally right, and *were determined* to act accordingly, it is obvious, that human laws, or even human organization to enforce God's laws, would be altogether unnecessary, and could serve no valuable purpose."—PRES. SHANNON: *Examiner,* No. 78.

**IMPERATIVE MOOD.**

The imperative mood is that form of the verb, which is used in commanding, exhorting, entreating, or permitting. It is commonly used only in the second person of the present tense.

**PRESENT TENSE.**

*Singular.* 2. Love [thou,] *or* Do thou love;

*Plural.* 2. Love [ye *or* you,] *or* Do you love.

OBS.—In the Greek language, which has three numbers, the imperative mood is used in the second and third persons of them all; and has also several different tenses, some of which cannot be clearly rendered in English. In Latin, this mood has a distinct form for the third person, both singular and plural. In Italian, Spanish, and French, the first person plural is also given it. Imitations of some of these forms are occasionally employed in English, particularly by the poets. Such imitations must be referred to this mood, unless by ellipsis and transposition we make them out to be something else; and against this there are strong objections. Again, as imprecation on one's self is not impossible, the first person singular may be added; so that this mood *may possibly have* all the persons and numbers. Examples: "*Come we* now to his translation of the Iliad."—*Pope's Pref. to Dunciad.* "*Proceed we* therefore in our subject."—*Ib.* "*Blessed be he* that blesseth thee."—*Gen.*, xxvii, 29. "Thy *kingdom come.*"—*Matt.*, vi, 10. "But *pass we* that."—*W. Scott.* "Third person: *Be he, Be they.*"—*Churchill's Gram.*, p. 92.

"My soul, *turn* from them—*turn we* to survey," &c.—*Goldsmith.*

"Then *turn we* to her latest tribune's name."—*Byron.*

"Where'er the eye could light these words you read:
'Who *comes* this way—*behold*, and *fear* to sin!'"—*Pollok.*

"*Fall he* that must, beneath his rival's arms,
And *live the rest*, secure of future harms."—*Pope.*

"*Cursed be I* that did so!—All the *charms*
Of Sycorax, toads, beetles, bats, *light* on you!"—*Shakspeare.*

"*Have done* thy charms, thou hateful wither'd hag!"—*Idem.*

**PARTICIPLES.**

1. *The Imperfect.* 2. *The Perfect.* 3. *The Preperfect.* Loving. Loved. Having loved.

**SYNOPSIS OF THE FIRST EXAMPLE.**

**FIRST PERSON SINGULAR.**

IND. I love *or* do love, I loved *or* did love, I have loved. I had loved, I shall *or* will love, I shall *or* will have loved. POT. I may, can, *or* must love; I might, could, would, *or* should love; I may, can, *or* must have loved; I might, could, would, *or* should have loved. SUBJ. If I love, If I loved.

**SECOND PERSON SINGULAR.**

IND. Thou lovest *or* dost love, Thou lovedst *or* didst love, Thou hast loved, Thou hadst loved, Thou shalt *or* wilt love, Thou shalt *or* wilt have loved. POT. Thou mayst, canst, *or* must love; Thou mightst, couldst, wouldst, *or* shouldst love; Thou mayst, canst, *or* must have loved; Thou mightst, couldst, wouldst *or* shouldst have loved. SUBJ. If thou love, If thou loved. IMP. Love [thou,] *or* Do thou love.

**THIRD PERSON SINGULAR.**

IND. He loves *or* does love, He loved *or* did love, He has loved, He had loved, He shall *or* will love, He shall *or* will have loved. POT. He may, can, *or* must love; He might, could, would, *or* should love; He may, can, *or* must have loved; He might, could, would, *or* should have loved. SUBJ. If he love, If he loved.

**FIRST PERSON PLURAL.**

IND. We love *or* do love, We loved *or* did loved, We have loved, We had loved, We shall *or* will love, We shall *or* will have loved. POT. We may, can, *or* must love, We might, could, would, *or* should love; We may, can, *or* must have loved; We might, could, would, *or* should have loved. SUBJ. If we love, If we loved.

**SECOND PERSON PLURAL.**

IND. You love *or* do love, You loved *or* did love, You have loved, You had loved, You shall *or* will love, You shall *or* will have loved. POT. You may, can, *or* must love; You might, could, would, *or* should love; You may, can, *or* must have loved; You might, could, would, *or* should have loved. SUBJ. If you love, If you loved. IMP. Love [ye *or* you,] *or* Do you love.

**THIRD PERSON PLURAL.**

IND. They love *or* do love, They loved *or* did love, They have loved, They had loved, They shall *or* will love, They shall *or* will have loved. POT. They may, can, *or* must love; They might, could, would, *or* should love; They may, can, *or* must have loved; They might, could, would, *or* should have loved. SUBJ. If they love, If they loved.

**FAMILIAR FORM WITH 'THOU.'**

NOTE.—In the familiar style, the second person singular of this verb, is usually and more properly formed thus:

IND. Thou lov'st *or* dost love, Thou loved *or* did love, Thou hast loved, Thou had loved, Thou shall *or* will love, Thou shall *or* will have loved. POT. Thou may, can, *or* must love; Thou might, could, would, *or* should love; Thou may, can, *or* must have loved; Thou might, could, would, *or* should have loved. SUBJ. If thou love, If thou loved. IMP. Love [thou,] *or* Do thou love.

**SECOND EXAMPLE.**

*The irregular active verb SEE, conjugated affirmatively.*

**PRINCIPAL PARTS.**

*Present. Preterit. Imp. Participle. Perf. Participle.* See. Saw. Seeing. Seen.

**INFINITIVE MOOD.**

PRESENT TENSE. To See.

PERFECT TENSE. To have seen.

**INDICATIVE MOOD.**

**PRESENT TENSE.**

*Singular.* 1. I see, 2. Thou seest, 3. He sees;

*Plural.* 1. We see, 2. You see, 3. They see.

**IMPERFECT TENSE.**

*Singular.* 1. I saw, 2. Thou sawest, 3. He saw;

*Plural.* 1. We saw, 2. You saw, 3. They saw.

**PERFECT TENSE.**

*Singular.* 1. I have seen, 2. Thou hast seen, 3. He has seen;

*Plural.* 1. We have seen, 2. You have seen, 3. They have seen.

**PLUPERFECT TENSE.**

*Singular.* 1. I had seen, 2. Thou hadst seen, He had seen;

*Plural.* 1. We had seen, 2. You had seen, 3. They had seen.

**FIRST-FUTURE TENSE.**

*Singular.* 1. I shall see, 2. Thou wilt see, He will see;

*Plural.* 1. We shall see, 2. You will see, 3. They will see.

**SECOND-FUTURE TENSE.**

*Singular.* 1. I shall have seen, 2. Thou wilt have seen, 3. He will have seen;

*Plural.* 1. We shall have seen, 2. You will have seen, 3. They will have seen.

**POTENTIAL MOOD.**

**PRESENT TENSE.**

*Singular.* 1. I may see, 2. Thou mayst see, 3. He may see;

*Plural.* 1. We may see, 2. You may see, 3. They may see.

**IMPERFECT TENSE.**

*Singular.* 1. I might see, 2. Thou mightst see, 3. He might see;

*Plural.* 1. We might see, 2. You might see, 3. They might see.

**PERFECT TENSE.**

*Singular.* 1. I may have seen, 2. Thou mayst have seen, 3. He may have seen;

*Plural.* 1. We may have seen, 2. You may have seen, 3. They may have seen.

**PLUPERFECT TENSE.**

*Singular.* 1. I might have seen, 2. Thou mightst have seen, 3. He might have seen;

*Plural.* 1. We might have seen, 2. You might have seen, 3. They might have seen.

**SUBJUNCTIVE MOOD.**

**PRESENT TENSE.**

*Singular.* 1. If I see, 2. If thou see, 3. If he see;

*Plural.* 1. If we see, 2. If you see, 3. If they see.

**IMPERFECT TENSE.**

*Singular.* 1. If I saw, 2. If thou saw, 3. If he saw;

*Plural.* 1. If we saw, 2. If you saw, 3. If they saw.

## IMPERATIVE MOOD.

**PRESENT TENSE.**

*Singular.* 2. See [thou,] *or* Do thou see; *Plural.* 2. See [ye *or* you,] *or* Do you see.

**PARTICIPLES.**

1. *The Imperfect.* 2. *The Perfect.* 3. *The Preperfect.*

Seeing. Seen. Having seen.

**NOTES.**

NOTE I—The student ought to be able to rehearse the form of a verb, not only according to the order of the entire conjugation, but also according to the synopsis of the several persons and numbers. One sixth part of the paradigm, thus recited, gives in general a fair sample of the whole: and, in class recitations, this mode of rehearsal will save much time: as, IND. I see *or* do see, I saw *or* did see, I have seen, I had seen, I shall *or* will see, I shall *or* will have seen. POT. I may, can, *or* must see; I might, could, would, *or* should see; I may, can, *or* must have seen; I might, could, would, *or* should have seen. SUBJ. If I see, If I saw.

NOTE II.—In the familiar style, the second person singular of this verb is usually and more properly formed thus: IND. Thou seest *or* dost see, Thou saw *or* did see, Thou hast seen, Thou had seen, Thou shall *or* will see, Thou shall *or* will have seen. POT. Thou may, can, *or* must see; Thou might, could, would, *or* should see; Thou may, can, *or* must have seen;

Thou might, could, would, *or* should have seen. SUBJ. If thou see, If thou saw. IMP. See [thou,] *or* Do thou see.

## THIRD EXAMPLE.

*The irregular neuter verb BE, conjugated affirmatively.*

**PRINCIPAL PARTS.**

*Present. Preterit. Imp. Participle. Perf. Participle.* Be. Was. Being. Been.

**INFINITIVE MOOD.**

PRESENT TENSE.
To be.

PERFECT TENSE.
To have been.

**INDICATIVE MOOD.**

**PRESENT TENSE.**

*Singular. Plural.* 1. I am, 1. We are, 2. Thou art, 2. You are, 3. He is; 3. They are.

**IMPERFECT TENSE.**

*Singular. Plural.* 1. I was, 1. We were, 2. Thou wast, (*or* wert,)[262] 2. You were, 3. He was; 3. They were.

PERFECT TENSE.

*Singular. Plural.* 1. I have been, 1. We have been, 2. Thou hast been, 2. You have been, 3. He has been; 3. They have been.

**PLUPERFECT TENSE.**

*Singular. Plural.* 1. I had been, 1. We had been, 2. Thou hadst been, 2. You had been, 3. He had been; 3. They had been.

**FIRST-FUTURE TENSE.**

*Singular. Plural.* 1. I shall be, 1. We shall be, 2. Thou wilt be, 2. You will be, 3. He will be; 3. They will be.

**SECOND-FUTURE TENSE.**

*Singular. Plural.* 1. I shall have been, 1. We shall have been, 2. Thou wilt have been, 2. You will have been, 3. He will have been; 3. They will have been.

**POTENTIAL MOOD.**

**PRESENT TENSE.**

*Singular. Plural.* 1. I may be, 1. We may be, 2. Thou mayst be, 2. You may be, 3. He may be, 3. They may be.

**IMPERFECT TENSE.**

*Singular. Plural.* 1. I might be, 1. We might be, 2. Thou mightst be, 2. You might be, 3. He might be; 3. They might be.

**PERFECT TENSE.**

*Singular.* *Plural.* 1. I may have been, 1. We may have been, 2. Thou mayst have been, 2. You may have been, 3. He may have been; 3. They may have been.

**PLUPERFECT TENSE.**

*Singular.* *Plural.* 1. I might have been, 1. We might have been, 2. Thou mightst have been, 2. You might have been, 3. He might have been; 3. They might have been.

**SUBJUNCTIVE MOOD.**

**PRESENT TENSE.**

*Singular.* *Plural.* 1. If I be, 1. If we be, 2. If thou be, 2. If you be, 3. If he be; 3. If they be.

**IMPERFECT TENSE.**

*Singular.* *Plural.* 1. If I were,[263] 1. If we were, 2. If thou were, *or* wert, [264] 2. If you were, 3. If he were; If they were.

**IMPERATIVE MOOD.**

**PRESENT TENSE.**

*Singular.* 2. Be [thou,] *or* Do thou be; *Plural.* 2. Be [ye *or* you,] *or* Do you be.

**PARTICIPLES.**

1. *The Imperfect.* 2. *The Perfect.* 3. *The Preperfect.* Being. Been. Having been.

**FAMILIAR FORM WITH 'THOU.'**

NOTE.—In the familiar style, the second person singular of this verb, is usually and more properly formed thus: IND. Thou art, Thou was, Thou hast been, Thou had been, Thou shall *or* will be, Thou shall *or* will have been. POT. Thou may, can, *or* must be; Thou might, could, would, *or* should be; Thou may, can, *or* must have been; Thou might, could, would, *or* should have been. SUBJ. If thou be, If thou were. IMP. Be [thou,] *or* Do thou be.

## OBSERVATIONS.

OBS. 1.—It appears that *be*, as well as *am*, was formerly used for the indicative present: as, "I be, Thou beest, He be; We be, Ye be, They be." See *Brightland's Gram.*, p. 114. Dr. Lowth, whose Grammar is still preferred at Harvard University, gives both forms, thus: "I am, Thou art, He is; We are, Ye are, They are. Or, I be, Thou beest, He *is*; We be, Ye be, They be." To the third person singular, he subjoins the following example and remark: "'I think it *be* thine indeed, for thou liest in it.' Shak. Hamlet. *Be*, in the singular number of this time and mode, especially in the third person, is obsolete; and *is become* somewhat antiquated *in the plural*."—*Lowth's Gram.*, p. 36. Dr. Johnson gives this tense thus: "*Sing.* I am; thou art; he is; *Plur.* We are, *or* be; ye are, *or* be; they are, *or* be." And adds, "The plural *be* is now little in use."—*Gram. in Johnson's Dict.*, p. 8. The Bible commonly has *am, art, is,* and *are*, but not always; the indicative *be* occurs in some places: as, "We *be* twelve brethren."—*Gen.*, xlii, 32. "What *be* these two olive branches?"—*Zech.*, iv, 12. Some traces of this usage still occur in poetry: as,

"There *be* more things to greet the heart and eyes
In Arno's dome of Art's most princely shrine,
Where Sculpture with her rainbow sister vies;

There *be* more marvels yet—but not for mine."
  —*Byron's Childe Harold*, Canto iv, st. 61.

OBS. 2.—Respecting the verb *wert*, it is not easy to determine whether it is most properly of the indicative mood only, or of the subjunctive mood only, or of both, or of neither. The *regular* and *analogical* form for the indicative, is "Thou *wast*;" and for the subjunctive, "If thou *were*." Brightland exhibits, "I *was* or *were*, Thou *wast* or *wert*, He *was* or *were*," without distinction of mood, for the three persons singular; and, for the plural, *were* only. Dr. Johnson gives us, for the indicative, "Thou wast, *or* wert;" with the remark, "*Wert* is properly of the *conjunctive* mood, and ought not to be used in the indicative."—*Johnson's Gram.*, p. 8. In his conjunctive (or subjunctive) mood, he has, "Thou *beest*," and "Thou *wert*." So Milton wrote, "If thou *beest* he."—*P. Lost*, B. i, l. 84. Likewise Shakspeare: "If thou *beest* Stephano."—*Tempest.* This inflection of *be* is obsolete: all now say, "If thou *be*." But *wert* is still in use, to some extent, *for both moods*; being generally placed by the grammarians in the subjunctive only, but much oftener written for the indicative: as, "Whate'er thou art or *wert*."—*Byron's Harold*, Canto iv, st. 115. "O thou that *wert* so happy!"—*Ib.*, st. 109. "Vainly *wert* thou wed."—*Ib.*, st. 169.

OBS. 3.—Dr. Lowth gave to this verb, BE, that form of the subjunctive mood, which it now has in most of our grammars; appending to it the following examples and questions: "'Before the sun, Before the Heavens, thou *wert*.'—*Milton.* 'Remember what thou *wert*.'—*Dryden.* 'I knew thou *wert* not slow to hear.'—*Addison.* 'Thou who of old *wert* sent to Israel's court.'—*Prior.* 'All this thou *wert*.'—*Pope.* 'Thou, Stella, *wert* no longer young.'—*Swift.* Shall we, in deference to these great authorities," asks the Doctor, "allow *wert* to be the same with *wast*, and common to the indicative and [the] subjunctive mood? or rather abide by the practice of our best ancient writers; the propriety of the language, which requires, as far as may be, distinct forms, for different moods; and the analogy of formation in each mood; I *was*, thou *wast*; I *were*, thou *wert*? all which conspire to make *wert* peculiar to the subjunctive mood."—*Lowth's Gram.*, p. 37; *Churchill's*, p. 251. I have before shown, that several of the "best ancient writers" *did not inflect* the verb *were*, but wrote "*thou were*;" and, surely, "the analogy of formation," requires that the subjunctive *be not inflected*. Hence "the propriety which requires distinct forms," requires not *wert*, in either mood. Why then should we make this contraction of the old indicative form *werest*, a *solitary exception*, by fixing it in the subjunctive only, and that in opposition to the best authorities that ever used it? It is worthier to take rank with its kindred *beest*, and be called an *archaism*.

OBS. 4.—The chief characteristical difference between the indicative and the subjunctive mood, is, that in the latter the verb is *not inflected at all*, in the different persons: IND. "Thou *magnifiest* his work." SUBJ. "Remember that thou *magnify* his work."—*Job*, xxxvi, 24. IND. "He *cuts* off, *shuts* up, and *gathers* together." SUBJ. "If he *cut* off, and *shut* up, or *gather* together, then who can hinder him?"—*Job*, xl, 10. There is also a difference of meaning. The Indicative, "If he *was*," admits the fact; the Subjunctive, "If he *were*," supposes that he was not. These moods may therefore be distinguished by the sense, even when their forms are alike: as, "Though *it thundered*, it did not rain."—"Though *it thundered*, he would not hear it." The indicative assumption here is, "Though it *did thunder*," or, "Though there *was thunder*;" the subjunctive, "Though it *should thunder*," or, "Though there *were* thunder." These senses are clearly different. Writers however are continually confounding these moods; some in one way, some in an other. Thus S. R. Hall, the teacher of a *Seminary for Teachers*: "SUBJ. *Present Tense*. 1. If I be, *or* am, 2. If thou be, *or* art, 3. If he be, *or* is; 1. If we be, *or* are, 2. If ye *or* you be, *or* are, 3. If they be, *or* are. *Imperfect Tense*. 1. If I were, *or* was, 2. If thou wert, *or* wast, 3. If he were, *or* was; 1. If we were, 2. If ye *or* you were, 3. If they were."—*Hall's Grammatical*

*Assistant*, p. 11. Again: "SUBJ. *Present Tense.* 1. If I love, 2. If thou *lovest*, 3. If he love," &c. "The remaining tenses of this *mode*, are, *in general*, similar to the correspondent tenses of the Indicative *mode, only* with the conjunction prefixed."—*Ib.*, p. 20. Dr. Johnson observes, "The indicative and conjunctive moods are by modern writers frequently confounded; or rather the conjunctive is wholly neglected, when some convenience of versification does not invite its revival. It is used among the purer writers of former times; as, 'Doubtless thou art our father, though Abraham *be* ignorant of us, and Israel *acknowledge* us not.'"—*Gram. in Joh. Dict.*, p. 9. To neglect the subjunctive mood, or to confound it with the indicative, is to augment several of the worst faults of the language.

## II. COMPOUND OR PROGRESSIVE FORM.

Active and neuter verbs may also be conjugated, by adding the Imperfect Participle to the auxiliary verb BE, through all its changes; as, "I *am writing* a letter."—"He *is sitting* idle."—"They *are going*." This form of the verb denotes a *continuance* of the action or state of being, and is, on many occasions, preferable to the simple form of the verb.

**FOURTH EXAMPLE.**

*The irregular active verb READ, conjugated affirmatively, in the Compound Form.*

**PRINCIPAL PARTS OF THE SIMPLE VERB.**

*Present. Preterit. Imp. Participle. Perf. Participle.* R=ead. R~ead. R=eading. R~ead.

**INFINITIVE MOOD.**

PRESENT TENSE.

To be reading.

PERFECT TENSE.

To have been reading.

**INDICATIVE MOOD.**

**PRESENT TENSE.**

*Singular. Plural.* 1. I am reading, 1. We are reading, 2. Thou art reading, 2. You are reading, 3. He is reading; 3. They are reading.

**IMPERFECT TENSE.**

*Singular. Plural.* 1. I was reading, 1. We were reading, 2. Thou wast reading, 2. You were reading, 3. He was reading; 3. They were reading.

**PERFECT TENSE.**

*Singular. Plural.* 1. I have been reading, 1. We have been reading, 2. Thou hast been reading, 2. You have been reading, 3. He has been reading; 3. They have been reading.

**PLUPERFECT TENSE.**

*Singular. Plural.* 1. I had been reading, 1. We had been reading, 2. Thou hadst been reading, 2. You had been reading, 3. He had been reading; 3. They had been reading.

**FIRST-FUTURE TENSE.**

*Singular. Plural.* 1. I shall be reading, 1. We shall be reading, 2. Thou wilt be reading, 2. You will be reading, 3. He will be reading; 3. They will be reading.

**SECOND-FUTURE TENSE.**

*Singular. Plural.* 1. I shall have been reading, 1. We shall have been reading, 2. Thou wilt have been reading, 2. You will have been reading, 3. He will have been reading; 3. They will have been reading.

**POTENTIAL MOOD.**

**PRESENT TENSE.**

*Singular. Plural.* 1. I may be reading, 1. We may be reading, 2. Thou mayst be reading, 2. You may be reading, 3. He may be reading; 3. They may be reading.

**IMPERFECT TENSE.**

*Singular. Plural.* 1. I might be reading, 1. We might be reading, 2. Thou mightst be reading, 2. You might be reading, 3. He might be reading; 3. They might be reading.

**PERFECT TENSE.**

*Singular. Plural.* 1. I may have been reading, 1. We may have been reading, 2. Thou mayst have been reading, 2. You may have been reading, 3. He may have been reading; 3. They may have been reading.

**PLUPERFECT TENSE.**

*Singular. Plural.* 1. I might have been reading, 1. We might have been reading, 2. Thou mightst have been reading, 2. You might have been reading, 3. He might have been reading; 3. They might have been reading.

**PRESENT TENSE.**

*Singular*. *Plural*. 1. If I be reading, 1. If we be reading, 2. If thou be reading, 2. If you be reading, 3. If he be reading; 3. If they be reading.

## IMPERFECT TENSE.

*Singular*. *Plural*. 1. If I were reading, 1. If we were reading, 2. If thou were reading, 2. If you were reading, 3. If he were reading; 3. If they were reading.

## IMPERATIVE MOOD.

Sing. 2. Be [thou] reading, *or* Do thou be reading;
Plur. 2. Be [ye or you] reading, *or* Do you be reading.

**PARTICIPLES.**

1. *The Imperfect*. 2. *The Perfect*. 3. *The Preperfect*. Being reading. —————- Having been reading.

## FAMILIAR FORM WITH 'THOU.'

NOTE.—In the familiar style, the second person singular of this verb, is usually and more properly formed thus: IND. Thou art reading, Thou was reading, Thou hast been reading, Thou had been reading, Thou shall *or* will be reading, Thou shall *or* will have been reading. POT. Thou may, can, *or* must be reading; Thou might, could, would, *or* should be reading; Thou may, can, *or* must have been reading; Thou might, could, would, *or* should have been reading. SUBJ. If thou be reading, If thou were reading. IMP. Be [thou,] reading, *or* Do thou be reading.

## OBSERVATIONS.

OBS. 1.—Those verbs which, in their simple form, imply continuance, do not admit the compound form: thus we say, "I *respect* him;" but not, "I *am respecting* him." This compound form seems to imply that kind of action, which is susceptible of intermissions and renewals. Affections of the mind or heart are supposed to last; or, rather, actions of this kind are complete as soon as they exist. Hence, *to love, to hate, to desire, to fear, to forget, to remember*, and many other such verbs, are *incapable* of this method of conjugation.[265] It is true, we often find in grammars such models, as, "I *was loving*, Thou *wast loving*, He *was loving*," &c. But this language, to express what the authors intend by it, is not English. "He *was loving*," can only mean, "He was *affectionate*:" in which sense, loving is an adjective, and susceptible of comparison. Who, in common parlance, has ever said, "He *was loving me*," or any thing like it? Yet some have improperly published various examples, or even whole conjugations, of this spurious sort. See such in *Adam's Gram.*, p. 91; *Gould's Adam*, 83; *Bullions's English Gram.*, 52; *his Analyt. and Pract. Gram.*, 92; *Chandler's New Gram.*, 85 and 86; *Clark's*, 80; *Cooper's Plain and Practical*, 70; *Frazee's Improved*, 66 and 69; *S. S. Greene's*, 234; *Guy's*, 25; *Hallock's*, 103; *Hart's*, 88; *Hendrick's*, 38; *Lennie's*, 31; *Lowth's*, 40; *Harrison's*, 34; *Perley's*, 36; *Pinneo's Primary*, 101.

OBS. 2.—Verbs of this form have sometimes a passive signification; as, "The books *are now selling*."—*Allen's Gram.*, p. 82. "As the money *was paying* down."—*Ainsworth's Dict., w.* As. "It requires no motion in the organs whilst it *is forming*."—*Murray's Gram.*, p. 8. "Those works *are long forming* which must always last."—*Dr. Chetwood*. "While the work of the temple *was carrying* on."—*Dr. J. Owen*. "The designs of Providence *are carrying* on."—*Bp. Butler*. "A scheme, which *has been carrying* on, and *is* still *carrying* on."—*Id., Analogy*, p. 188. "We are permitted to know nothing of what *is transacting* in the regions above us."—*Dr. Blair*. "While these things *were transacting* in Germany."—*Russell's Modern Europe*, Part First, Let. 59. "As he *was carrying* to execution, he demanded to be heard."—*Goldsmith's Greece*, Vol. i, p. 163. "To declare that the action *was doing* or done."—*Booth's Introd.*, p. 28. "It *is doing* by thousands now."—*Abbott's Young Christian*, p. 121. "While the experiment *was making*, he was watching every movement."—*Ib.*, p. 309. "A series of communications from heaven, which *had been making* for fifteen hundred years."—*Ib.*, p. 166. "Plutarch's Lives *are re-printing*."—*L. Murray's Gram.*, 8vo, p. 64. "My Lives *are reprinting*."—DR. JOHNSON: *Worcester's Univ. and Crit. Dict.*, p. xlvi. "All this *has been transacting* within 130 miles of London."—BYRON: *Perley's Gram.*, p. 37. "When the heart *is corroding* by vexations."—*Student's Manual*, p. 336. "The padlocks for our lips *are forging*."—WHITTIER: *Liberator*, No. 993. "When his throat *is cutting*."—*Collier's Antoninus*. "While your story *is telling*."—*Adams's Rhet.*, i, 425. "But the seeds of it *were sowing* some time before."—*Bolingbroke, on History*, p. 168. "As soon as it was formed, nay even whilst it *was forming*."—*Ib.*, p. 163. "Strange schemes of private ambition *were formed and forming* there."—*Ib.*, p. 291. "Even when it *was making and made*."—*Ib.*, 299. "Which have been made and *are making*."—HENRY CLAY: *Liberator*, ix, p. 141. "And they are in measure *sanctified*, or *sanctifying*, by the power thereof."—*Barclay's Works*, i, 537. "Which *is* now *accomplishing* amongst the uncivilized countries of the earth."—*Chalmers, Sermons*, p. 281. "Who *are ruining*, or *ruined*, [in] this way."—*Locke, on Ed.*, p. 155. "Whilst they *were undoing*."—*Ibid.* "Whether he was employing fire to consume [something,] or *was* himself *consuming* by fire."—*Crombie, on*

*Etym. and Syntax*, p. 148. "At home, the greatest exertions *are making* to promote its progress."—*Sheridan's Elocution*, p. iv. "With those [sounds] which *are uttering*."—*Ib.*, p. 125. "Orders *are now concerting* for the dismissal of all officers of the Revenue marine."—*Providence Journal*, Feb. 1, 1850. Expressions of this kind are condemned by some critics, under the notion that the participle in *ing* must never be passive; but the usage is unquestionably of far better authority, and, according to my apprehension, in far better taste, than the more complex phraseology which some late writers adopt in its stead; as, "The books *are* now *being sold*."—"In all the towns about Cork, the whiskey shops *are being closed*, and soup, coffee, and tea houses [are] *establishing* generally."—*Dublin Evening Post*, 1840.

OBS. 3.—The question here is, Which is the most correct expression, "While the bridge *was building*,"—"While the bridge was *a* building,"—or, "While the bridge *was being built*?" And again, Are they all wrong? If none of these is right, we must reject them all, and say, "While *they were building* the bridge;"—"While the bridge *was in process of erection*;"—or resort to some other equivalent phrase. Dr. Johnson, after noticing the compound form of active-intransitives, as, "I *am going*"—"She *is dying*,"—"The tempest *is raging*,"—"I *have been walking*," and so forth, adds: "There is another manner of using the active participle, which gives it a *passive* signification:[266] as, The grammar is now printing, *Grammatica jam nunc chartis imprimitur*. The brass is forging, *Æra excuduntur*. This is, in my opinion," says he, "a *vitious* expression, probably corrupted from a phrase more pure, but now somewhat obsolete: The book is *a* printing, The brass is *a* forging; *a* being properly *at*, and *printing* and *forging* verbal nouns signifying action, according to the analogy of this language."—*Gram. in Joh. Dict.*, p. 9.

OBS. 4.—*A* is certainly sometimes a *preposition*; and, as such, it may govern a participle, and that without converting it into a "*verbal noun*." But that such phraseology ought to be preferred to what is exhibited with so many authorities, in a preceding paragraph, and with an example from Johnson among the rest, I am not prepared to concede. As to the notion of introducing a new and more complex passive form of conjugation, as, "The bridge is *being built*," "The bridge *was being built*," and so forth, it is one of the most absurd and monstrous innovations ever thought of. Yet some two or three men, who seem to delight in huge absurdities, declare that this "modern *innovation* is *likely to supersede*" the simpler mode of expression. Thus, in stead of, "The work *is now publishing*," they choose to say, "The work is *now being published*."—*Kirkham's Gram.*, p. 82. This is certainly no better English than, "The work *was being published, has been being published, had been being published, shall or will be being published, shall or will have been being published*;" and so on, through all the moods and tenses. What a language shall we have when our verbs are thus conjugated!

OBS. 5.—A certain *Irish* critic, who even outdoes in rashness the above-cited American, having recently arrived in New York, has republished a grammar, in which he not only repudiates the passive use of the participle in *ing*, but denies the usual passive form of the present tense, "*I am loved, I am smitten*" &c., as taught by Murray and others, to be good English; and tells us that the true form is, "*I am being loved, I am being smitten*," &c. See the 98th and 103d pages of *Joseph W. Wright's Philosophical Grammar*, (*Edition of* 1838,) *dedicated* "TO COMMON SENSE!" [267] But both are offset, if not refuted, by the following observations from a source decidedly better: "It has lately become common to use the present participle passive [,] to express the suffering of an action as *continuing*, instead of the participle in *-ing* in the passive sense; thus, instead of, 'The house *is building*,' we now very frequently hear, 'The house *is being built*.' This mode of expression, besides being awkward, is incorrect, and *does not*

"1. The expression, '*is being*,' is equivalent to '*is*,' and expresses no more; just as, '*is loving*,' is equivalent to, '*loves*.' Hence, '*is being built*,' is precisely equivalent to, '*is built*.'

"2. '*Built*,' is a perfect participle; and therefore cannot, in any connexion, express an action, or the suffering of an action, *now in progress*. The verb *to be*, signifies *to exist*; '*being*,' therefore, is equivalent to '*existing*.' If then we substitute the synonyme, the nature of the expression will be obvious; thus, 'the house is *being built*,' is, in other words, 'the house is *existing built*,' or more simply as before, 'the house *is built*;' plainly importing an action not progressing, but now *existing in a finished state*.

"3. If the expression, '*is being built*,' be a correct form of the present indicative passive, then it must be equally correct to say in the perfect, '*has been being built*;' in the past perfect, '*had been being built*;' in the present infinitive,'*to be being built*;' in the perfect infinitive,'*to have been being built*;' and in the present participle, '*being being built*;' which all will admit to be expressions as incorrect as they are inelegant, but precisely analogous to that which now begins to prevail."—*Bullions's Principles of English Gram.*, p. 58.

OBS. 6.—It may be replied, that the verbs *to be* and *to exist* are not always synonymous; because the former is often a mere auxiliary, or a mere copula, whereas the latter always means something positive, as *to be in being, to be extant*. Thus we may speak of a thing as *being destroyed*, or may say, it *is annihilated*; but we can by no means speak of it as *existing destroyed*, or say, it *exists annihilated*. The first argument above is also nugatory. These drawbacks, however, do not wholly destroy the force of the foregoing criticism, or at all extenuate the obvious tautology and impropriety of such phrases as, *is being, was being*, &c. The gentlemen who affirm that this new form of conjugation "*is being introduced* into the language," (since they allow participles to follow possessive pronouns) may very fairly be asked, "What evidence have you of *its being being introduced*?" Nor can they, on their own principles, either object to the monstrous phraseology of this question, or tell how to better it![268]

OBS. 7.—D. H. Sanborn, an other recent writer, has very emphatically censured this innovation, as follows: "English and American writers have of late introduced a new kind of phraseology, which has become quite prevalent in the periodical and popular publications of the day. Their intention, doubtless, is, to supersede the use of the verb in the *definite form*, when it has a passive signification. They say, 'The ship is *being* built,'—'time is *being wasted*,"—'the work is *being advanced*,' instead of, 'the ship is *building*, time is *wasting*, the work is *advancing*.' Such a phraseology is a solecism too palpable to receive any favor; it is at war with the practice of the most distinguished writers in the English language, such as Dr. Johnson and Addison. "When an individual says, 'a house is being burned,' he declares that a house is *existing, burned*, which is impossible; for *being* means existing, and *burned, consumed by fire*. The house ceases to exist as such, after it is consumed by fire. But when he says, 'a house *is burning*,' we understand that it is *consuming by fire*; instead of inaccuracy, doubt, and ambiguity, we have a form of expression perfectly intelligible, beautiful, definite, and appropriate."—*Sanborn's Analytical Gram.*, p. 102.

OBS. 8.—Dr. Perley speaks of this usage thus: "An attempt has been made of late to introduce a kind of passive participial voice; as, 'The temple is being built.' This ought not to be encouraged. For, besides being an innovation, it is less convenient than the use of the present participle in the passive sense. *Being built* signifies action *finished*; and how can, *Is being built*, signify an *action unfinished?*"—*Perley's Gram.*, p. 37.

OBS. 9.—The question now before us has drawn forth, on either side, a deal of ill scholarship and false logic, of which it would be tedious to give even a synopsis. Concerning the import of some of our most common words and phrases, these ingenious masters,—Bullions, Sanborn, and Perley,—severally assert some things which seem not to be exactly true. It is remarkable that critics can err in expounding terms so central to the language, and so familiar to all ears, as "*be, being, being built, burned, being burned, is, is burned, to be burned,*" and the like. *That to be* and *to exist*, or their like derivatives, such as *being* and *existing, is* and *exists*, cannot always explain each other, is sufficiently shown above; and thereby is refuted Sanborn's chief argument, that, "*is being burned,*" involves the contradiction of "*existing, burned,*" or "*consumed by fire.*" According to his reasoning, as well as that of Bullions, *is burned* must mean *exists consumed; was burned, existed consumed*; and thus our whole passive conjugation would often be found made up of bald absurdities! That this new *unco-passive* form conflicts with the older and better usage of taking the progressive form sometimes passively, is doubtless a good argument against the innovation; but that "Johnson and Addison" are fit representatives of the older "practice" in this case, may be doubted. I know not that the latter has anywhere made use of such phraseology; and one or two examples from the former are scarcely an offset to his positive verdict against the usage. See OBS. 3rd, above.

OBS. 10.—As to what is called "*the present* or *the imperfect participle passive,*"—as, "*being burned,*" or "*being burnt,*"—if it is rightly interpreted in *any* of the foregoing citations, it is, beyond question, very improperly *thus* named. In participles, *ing* denotes *continuance*: thus *being* usually means *continuing to be; loving, continuing to love; building, continuing to build*,—or (as taken passively) *continuing to be built*: i. e., (in words which express the sense more precisely and certainly,) *continuing to be in process of construction*. What then is "being built," but "*continuing to be built,*" the same, or nearly the same, as "*building*" taken passively? True it is, that *built*, when alone, being a perfect participle, does not mean "*in process of construction*," but rather, "*constructed*" which intimates *completion*; yet, in the foregoing passive phrases, and others like them, as well as in all examples of this unco-passive voice, continuance of the passive state being first suggested, and cessation of the act being either regarded as future or disregarded, the imperfect participle passive is for the most part received as equivalent to the simple imperfect used in a passive sense. But Dr. Bullions, who, after making "*is being built* precisely equivalent to *is built*," classes the two participles differently, and both erroneously,—the one as a "*present* participle," and the other, of late, as a "*past*,"—has also said above, "'*Built*,' is a *perfect* participle: and THEREFORE cannot, in *any connexion*, express an action, or the suffering of an action, *now in progress*." And Dr. Perley, who also calls the compound of *being* a "*present* participle," argues thus: "*Being built* signifies an *action, finished*; and how can *Is being built*, signify an *action unfinished*?" To expound a *passive* term *actively*, or as "signifying *action*," is, at any rate, a near approach to absurdity; and I shall presently show that the fore-cited notion of "a perfect participle," now half abandoned by Bullions himself, has been the seed of the very worst form of that ridiculous neology which the good Doctor was opposing.

OBS. 11.—These criticisms being based upon the *meaning* of certain participles, either alone or in phrases, and the particular terms spoken of being chiefly meant to represent *classes*, what is said of them may be understood of their *kinds*. Hence the appropriate *naming* of the kinds, so as to convey no false idea of any participle's import, is justly brought into view; and I may be allowed to say here, that, for the first participle passive, which begins with "*being*," the epithet "*Imperfect*" is better than "*Present*," because this compound participle denotes, not always what is *present*, but always *the state* of something by which an action is, *or was, or will be, undergone or undergoing—a state continuing,* or so regarded, though perhaps the action causative may be ended—or sometimes perhaps imagined only, and not yet really begun. With a marvellous instability of doctrine, for the professed systematizer of different languages and grammars, Dr. Bullions has recently changed his names of the second and third participles, in both voices, from "*Perfect*" and "*Compound Perfect*," to "*Past*" and "*Perfect.*" His notion now is, that, "*The Perfect* participle is always compound; as, *Having finished, Having been finished.*"—*Bullions's Analyt. and Pract. Grammar*, 1849, p. 77. And what was the "*Perfect*" before, in his several books, is now called the "*Past*;" though, with this change, he has deliberately made an other which is repugnant to it: this participle, being the basis of three tenses always, and of all the tenses sometimes, is now allowed by the Doctor to lend the term "*perfect*" to the three,—"*Present-perfect, Past-perfect, Future-perfect,*"—even when itself is named otherwise!

OBS. 12.—From the erroneous conception, that a perfect participle must, in every connexion, express "*action finished,*" *action past,*—or perhaps from only a moiety of this great error,—the notion that such a participle cannot, in connexion with an auxiliary, constitute a passive verb of the *present tense,*—J. W. Wright, above-mentioned, has not very unnaturally reasoned, that, "The expression, '*I am loved,*' which Mr. Murray has employed to exhibit the passive conjugation of the *present tense*, may much more *feasibly* represent *past* than *present* time."—See *Wright's Philosophical Gram.*, p. 99. Accordingly, in his own paradigm of the passive verb, he has formed *this* tense solely from what he calls the participle *present*, thus: "I *am being smitten*, Thou *art being smitten*," &c.—*Ib.*, p. 98. His "*Passed Tense,*" too, for some reason which I do not discover, he distinguishes above the rest by a *double form*, thus: "I *was smitten, or being smitten*; Thou *wast smitten, or being smitten*;" &c.—P. 99. In his opinion, "Few will object to *the propriety of* the more familiar phraseology, '*I am in the* ACT,—or, *suffering* the ACTION *of* BEING SMITTEN;' and yet," says he, "in substance and effect, it is wholly the same as, '*I am being smitten*,' which is THE TRUE FORM of the verb in the *present* tense of the *passive voice!*"—*Ibid.* Had we not met with some similar expressions of English or American blunderers, "the *act* or *action of being smitten*," would be accounted a downright Irish bull; and as to this ultra notion of neologizing all our passive verbs, by the addition of "*being*,"—with the author's cool talk of "*the presentation of this theory, and* [*the*] *consequent suppression of that hitherto employed*,"—there is a transcendency in it, worthy of the most sublime aspirant among grammatical newfanglers.

OBS. 13.—But, with all its boldness of innovation, Wright's Philosophical Grammar is not a little *self-contradictory* in its treatment of the passive verb. The entire "suppression" of the usual form of its present tense, did not always appear, even to this author, quite so easy and reasonable a matter, as the foregoing citations would seem to represent it. The passive use of the participle in *ing*, he has easily disposed of: despite innumerable authorities for it, one false assertion, of seven syllables, suffices to make it quite impossible.[269] But the usual passive form, which, with some show of truth, is accused of not having always precisely the same meaning as the progressive used passively,—that is, of not always denoting *continuance in the state of receiving continued action*,—and which is, for that remarkable reason, judged worthy of *rejection*, is nevertheless admitted to have, in very many instances, a conformity to this idea, and therefore to "belong [thus far] to the present tense."—P. 103. This contradicts to an indefinite extent, the proposition for its rejection. It is observable also, that the same examples, '*I am loved*' and 'I *am smitten*,'—the same "*tolerated, but erroneous forms*," (so called on page 103,) that are given as specimens of what he would reject,—though at first pronounced "*equivalent* in grammatical construction," censured for the same pretended error, and proposed to be changed alike to "*the true form*" by the insertion of "*being*,"—are subsequently declared to "belong to" different classes and different tenses. "*I am loved,*" is referred to that "numerous" class of verbs, which "*detail* ACTION *of prior, but retained, endured, and continued existence*; and therefore, in this sense, *belong to the present tense.*" But "*I am smitten,*" is idly reckoned of an opposite class, (said by Dr. Bullions to be "perhaps the greater number,") whose "ACTIONS described are neither *continuous* in their nature, nor *progressive* in their duration; but, on the contrary, *completed* and *perfected*; and [which] are consequently descriptive of *passed* time and ACTION."—*Wright's Gram.*, p. 103. Again: "In what instance soever this latter form and signification *can* be introduced, *their import should be, and, indeed, ought to be, supplied by the perfect tense construction*:—for example, '*I am smitten,*' [should] be, '*I have been smitten.*'"—*Ib.* Here is self-contradiction indefinitely extended *in an other way*. Many a good phrase, if not every one, that the author's first suggestion would turn to the unco-passive form, his present "*remedy*" would about as absurdly convert into "the perfect tense."

OBS. 14.—But Wright's inconsistency, about this matter, ends not here: it runs through all he says of it; for, in this instance, error and inconsistency constitute his whole story. In one place, he anticipates and answers a question thus: "To what tense do the constructions, 'I am pleased;' 'He is expected;' '*I am smitten*;' 'He is bound;' belong?" "We answer:—*So far as* these and like constructions are applicable to the delineation of *continuous* and *retained* ACTION, they express *present* time; and must be treated accordingly."—P. 103. This seems to intimate that even, "*I am smitten,*" and its likes, as they stand, may have some good claim to be of the present tense; which suggestion is contrary to several others made by the author. To expound this, or any other passive term, *passively*, never enters his mind: with him, as with sundry others, "ACTION," "*finished* ACTION," or "*progressive* ACTION," is all any *passive* verb or participle ever means! No marvel, that awkward perversions of the forms of utterance and the principles of grammar should follow such interpretation. In Wright's syntax a very queer distinction is apparently made between a passive verb, and the participle chiefly constituting it; and here, too, through a fancied ellipsis of "*being*" before the latter, most, if not all, of his other positions concerning passives, are again disastrously overthrown by something worse—a word "*imperceptibly understood*." "'*I am smitten*;' '*I was smitten*;' &c., are," he says, "the *universally acknowledged forms* of the VERBS in these tenses, in the passive voice:—not of the *PARTICIPLE*. In all verbal constructions of the character of which we have hitherto treated, (see page 103) *and, where* the ACTIONS described are *continuous* in their *operations*,—the participle BEING is *imperceptibly omitted, by ellipsis*."—P. 144.

OBS. 15.—Dr. Bullions has stated, that, "The present participle active, and the present participle passive, are *not counterparts* to each other in signification; [,] the one signifying the present doing, and the other the present suffering of an action, [;] for the latter *always intimates the present being of an* ACT, *not in progress, but completed*."—*Prin. of Eng. Gram.*, p. 58. In this, he errs no less grossly than in his idea of the "*action* or the suffering" expressed by "a *perfect* participle," as cited in OBS. 5th above; namely, that it must have *ceased*. Worse interpretation, or balder absurdity, is scarcely to be met with; and yet the reverend Doctor, great linguist as he should be, was here only trying to think and tell the common import of a very common sort of *English* participles; such as, "*being loved*" and "*being seen*." In grammar, "*an act*," that has "*present being*," can be nothing else than an act now doing, or "*in progress*;" and if, "*the present being of an* ACT *not in progress*," were here a possible thought, it surely could not be intimated by any *such* participle. In Acts, i, 3 and 4, it is stated, that our Saviour showed himself to the apostles, "alive after his passion, by many infallible proofs, *being seen* of them forty days, and *speaking* of the things *pertaining* to the kingdom of God; and, *being assembled* together with them commanded them that they should not depart from Jerusalem." Now, of these misnamed "*present* participles," we have here one "*active*," one "*passive*," and two others—(one in each form—) that are *neuter*; but *no present time*, except what is in the indefinite date of "*pertaining*." The events are past, and were so in the days of St. Luke. Yet each of the participles denotes *continuance*: not, indeed, in or to the *present time*, but *for a time*. "*Being seen*" means *continuing to be seen*; and, in this instance, the period of the continuance was "forty days" of time past. But, according to the above-cited "*principle of English Grammar*," so long and so widely inculcated by "the Rev. Peter Bullions, D. D., Professor of Languages," &c., —a central principle of interpretation, presumed by him to hold "*always*"— this participle must intimate "*the present being of an act, not in progress, but completed*;"—that is, "*the present being of*" the apostles' act in formerly *seeing the risen Saviour*!

OBS. 16.—This grammarian has lately taken a deal of needless pains to sustain, by a studied division of verbs into two classes, similar to those which are mentioned in OBS. 13th above, a part of the philosophy of J. W. Wright, concerning our usual form of passives in the present tense. But, as he now will have it, that the two voices sometimes tally as counterparts, it is plain that he adheres but partially to his former erroneous conception of a perfect or "past" participle, and the terms which hold it "in any connexion." The awkward substitutes proposed by the Irish critic, he does not indeed countenance; but argues against them still, and, in some respects, very justly. The doctrine now common to these authors, on this point, is the highly important one, that, in respect to half our verbs, what we commonly take for the passive present, *is not such*—that, in "the *second* class, (perhaps the greater number,) the *present-passive* implies that *the act expressed by the active voice has ceased*. Thus, 'The house is built.' * * * Strictly speaking, then," says the Doctor, "the PAST PARTICIPLE with the verb TO BE *is not the present tense in the passive voice of verbs thus used*; that is, this form does not express passively the *doing* of the act."—*Bullions's Analyt. and Pract. Grammar*, Ed. of 1849, p. 235. Thus far these two authors agree; except that Wright seems to have avoided the incongruity of *calling* that "*the present-passive*" which he *denies* to be such. But the Doctor, approving none of this practitioner's "remedies," and being less solicitous to provide other treatment than expulsion for the thousands of present passives which both deem spurious, adds, as from the chair, this verdict: "These verbs either *have no present-passive*, or it is made by annexing the participle in *ing*, in its passive sense, to the verb *to be*; as, 'The house *is building*.'"—*Ib.*, p. 236.

OBS. 17.—It would seem, that Dr. Bullions thinks, and in reality Wright also, that nothing can be a present passive, but what "*expresses passively the* DOING *of the act.*" This is about as wise, as to try to imagine every active verb to *express actively the receiving of an act*! It borders exceedingly hard upon absurdity; it very much resembles the nonsense of "*expressing receptively the giving of something*!" Besides, the word "DOING," being used substantively, does not determine well what is here meant; which is, I suppose, *continuance*, or an *unfinished state* of the act received—an idea which seems adapted to the participle in *ing*, but which it is certainly no fault of a participle ending in *d, t,* or *n*, not to suggest. To "*express passively the doing of the act*," if the language means any thing rational, may be, simply to say, that the act *is* or *was done*. For "*doings*" are, as often as any-wise, "*things done*," as *buildings* are *fabrics built*; and "*is built*," and "*am smitten*," the gentlemen's choice examples of *false passives*, and of "*actions finished*,"—though neither of them necessarily intimates either continuance or cessation of the act suffered, or, if it did, would be the less or the more passive or present,—may, in such a sense, "express *the doing* of the act," if any passives can:—nay, the "finished act" has such completion as may be stated with degrees of progress or of frequency; as, "The house *is partly built*."—"I *am oftener smitten*." There is, undoubtedly, some difference between the assertions, "The house *is building*,"—and, "The house *is partly built*;" though, for practical purposes, perhaps, we need not always be very nice in choosing between them. For the sake of variety, however, if for nothing else, it is to be hoped, the doctrine above-cited, which limits half our passive verbs of the present tense, *to the progressive form only*, will not soon be generally approved. It impairs the language more than unco-passives are likely ever to corrupt it.

OBS. 18.—"No *startling novelties* have been introduced," says the preface to the "Analytical and Practical Grammar of the English Language." To have shunned all shocking innovations, is only to have exercised common prudence. It is not pretended, that any of the Doctor's errors here remarked upon, or elsewhere in this treatise, will *startle* any body; but, if errors exist, even in plausible guise, it may not be amiss, if I tell of them. To suppose every verb or participle to be either "*transitive*" or "*intransitive,*" setting all *passives* with the former sort, all *neuters* with the latter; (p. 59;) —to define the *transitive* verb or participle as expressing always "*an act DONE by one person or thing to another;*" (p. 60;)—to say, after making passive verbs transitive, "The object of a transitive verb is in the *objective case,*" and, "A verb that does not make sense with an objective after it, is intransitive;" (p. 60;)—to insist upon a precise and almost universal *identity of "meaning"* in terms so obviously *contrasted* as are the two voices, "active" and "passive;" (pp. 95 and 235;)—to allege, as a general principle, "that whether we use the active, or the passive voice, *the meaning is the same,* except in some cases in the present tense;" (p. 67;)—to attribute to the forms naturally opposite in voice and sense, that sameness of meaning which is observable only in certain *whole sentences* formed from them; (pp. 67, 95, and 235;)—to assume that each "VOICE is a particular *form of the verb,*" yet make it include *two cases,* and often a preposition before one of them; (pp. 66, 67, and 95;)—to pretend from the words, "The PASSIVE VOICE represents the subject of the verb as *acted upon,*" (p. 67,) that, "*According to the* DEFINITION, the passive voice expresses, passively, *the same thing* that the active does actively;" (p. 235;)—to affirm that, "'Cæsar *conquered* Gaul,' and 'Gaul *was conquered* by Cæsar,' express *precisely the same idea,*"—and then say, "It will be felt at once that the expressions, 'Cæsar *conquers* Gaul,' and 'Gaul *is conquered* by Cæsar,' *do not express the same thing;*" (p. 235;)—to deny that passive verbs or neuter are worthy to constitute a distinct class, yet profess to find, in one single tense of the former, such a difference of meaning as warrants a general division of verbs in respect to it; (*ib.*;)—to announce, in bad English, that, "*In regard to this matter* [,] there are evidently Two CLASSES of verbs; namely, those *whose* present-passive expresses precisely the same thing, passively, as the active voice does actively, and those *in which it* does not:" (*ib.*;)—to do these several things, as they have been done, is, to set forth, not "novelties" only, but errors and inconsistencies.

OBS. 19.—Dr. Bullions still adheres to his old argument, that *being* after its own verb must be devoid of meaning; or, in his own words, "that *is being built,* if it mean anything, can mean nothing more than *is built,* which is not the idea intended to be expressed."—*Analyt. and Pract. Gram.*, p. 237. He had said, (as cited in OBS. 5th above,) "The expression, '*is being,*' is equivalent to *is,* and expresses *no more*; just as, '*is loving,*' is equivalent to '*loves.*' Hence, '*is being built,*' is precisely equivalent to '*is built.*'"—*Principles of E. Gram.*, p. 58. He has now discovered "that *there is no progressive form* of the verb *to be,* and no need of it:" and that, "hence, *there is no such expression* in English as *is being.*"—*Analyt. and Pract. Gram.*, p. 236. He should have noticed also, that "*is loving*" is not an authorized "equivalent to *loves*;" and, further, that the error of saying "*is being built,*" is only in the relation of the *first two words* to each other. If "*is being,*" and "*is loving,*" are left unused for the same reason, the truth may be, that *is* itself, like *loves,* commonly denotes "*continuance*;" and that *being* after it, in stead of being necessary or proper, can only be awkwardly tautologous. This is, in fact, THE GRAND OBJECTION to the new phraseology—"*is being practised*"—"*am being smitten*"—and the like.

Were there no danger that petty writers would one day seize upon it with like avidity, an other innovation, exactly similar to this in every thing but tense—similar in awkwardness, in tautology, in unmistakeableness—might here be uttered for the sake of illustration. Some men conceive, that "The *perfect* participle is always compound; as, *having seen, having written*;"—and that the simple word, *seen* or *written*, had originally, and still ought to have, only a passive construction. For such views, they find authorities. Hence, in lieu of the common phrases, "*had we seen*," "*we have written*," they adopt such English as this; "*Had we having seen* you, we should have stopped."—"*We have having written* but just now, to our correspondent." Now, "*We are being smitten*," is no better grammar than this;—and no worse: "The idea intended" is in no great jeopardy in either case.

OBS. 20.—J. R. Chandler, of Philadelphia, in his Common School Grammar of 1847, has earnestly undertaken the *defence* of this new and much-mooted passive expression: which he calls "*the Definite Passive Voice*," or "*the Passive Voice of the Definite Form*." He admits it, however, to be a form that "does not *sound well*,"—a "*novelty* that strikes the ear unpleasantly;" but he will have the defect to be, not in the tautologous conceit of "*is being*," "*was being*," "*has been being*," and the like, but in everybody's organ of hearing,—supposing all ears corrupted, "from infancy," to a distaste for correct speech, by "the habit of *hearing* and using words *ungrammatically*!"—See p. 89. Claiming this new form as "*the true passive*," in just contrast with the progressive active, he not only rebukes all attempts "to evade" the use of it, "by some real or supposed *equivalent*," but also declares, that, "The attempt to deprive the transitive definite verb of [this] *its passive voice, is to strike at the foundation of the language*, and *to strip it of one of its most important qualities*; that of making both actor and sufferer, each in turn and at pleasure, the subject of conversation."—*Ibid.* Concerning *equivalents*, he evidently argues fallaciously; for he urges, that the using of them "*does not dispense with the necessity of the definite passive voice*."—P. 88. But it is plain, that, of the many fair substitutes which may in most cases be found, if any one is preferred, this form, and all the rest, are of course rejected for the time.

OBS. 21.—By Chandler, as well as others, this new passive form is justified only on the supposition, that the simple participle in *ing* can never with propriety be used passively. No plausible argument, indeed, can be framed for it, without the assumption, that the simpler form, when used in the same sense, *is ungrammatical*. But this is, in fact, a begging of the main question; and that, in opposition to abundant authority for the usage condemned. (See OBS. 3d, above.) This author pretends that, "*The RULE of all grammarians* declares the verb *is*, and a *present participle* (*is building*, or *is writing*), to be in the active voice" only.—P. 88. (I add the word "*only*," but this is what he means, else he merely quibbles.) Now in this idea he is wrong, and so are the several grammarians who support the principle of this imaginary "*RULE*." The opinion of critics in general would be better represented by the following suggestions of the Rev. W. Allen: "When the English verb does not signify *mental affection*, the distinction of voice is often disregarded: thus we say, *actively*, they *were selling* fruit; and, *passively*, the books *are* now *selling*. The same remark applies to the participle used as a noun: as, actively, *drawing* is an elegant amusement, *building* is expensive; and, passively, his *drawings* are good, this is a fine building."—*Allen's Elements of E. Gram.*, p. 82.

OBS. 22.—Chandler admits, that, "When it is said, 'The house is *building*,' the meaning is easily obtained; though," he strangely insists, "*it is exactly opposite to the assertion*."—P. 89. He endeavours to show, moreover, by a fictitious example made for the purpose, that the progressive form, if used in both voices, will be liable to ambiguity. It may, perhaps, be so in some instances; but, were there weight enough in the objection to condemn the passive usage altogether, one would suppose there might be found, somewhere, *an actual example or two* of the abuse. Not concurring with Dr. Bullions in the notion that the active voice and the passive usually "express precisely the same thing," this critic concludes his argument with the following sentence: "There is an *important difference* between *doing* and *suffering*; and that *difference is grammatically shown* by the appropriate use of the active and passive voices of a verb."—*Chandler's Common School Gram.*, p. 89.

OBS. 23.—The opinion given at the close of OBS. 2d above, was first published in 1833. An opposite doctrine, with the suggestion that it is "*improper* to say, '*the house is building*,' instead of 'the house *is being built*,'"—is found on page 64th of the Rev. David Blair's Grammar, of 1815, —"Seventh Edition," with a preface dated, "*October 20th*, 1814." To any grammarian who wrote at a period much earlier than that, the question about *unco-passives* never occurred. Many critics have passed judgement upon them since, and so generally with reprobation, that the man must have more hardihood than sense, who will yet disgust his readers or hearers with them.[270] That "This new form has been used by *some respectable writers*," we need not deny; but let us look at the given "*instances of it*: 'For those who *are being educated* in our seminaries.' R. SOUTHEY.—'It *was being uttered*.' COLERIDGE.—'The foundation *was being laid*.' BRIT. CRITIC."—*English Grammar with Worcester's Univ. and Crit. Dict.*, p. xlvi. Here, for the first example, it would be much better to say, "For those who *are educated*," [271]—or, "who *are receiving their education*;" for the others, "It *was uttering*,"—"*was uttered*,"—or, "*was in uttering*."—"The foundation *was laying*,"—"*was laid*,"—or, "*was about being laid*." Worcester's opinion of the "new form" is to be inferred from his manner of naming it in the following sentence: "Within a few years, a *strange and awkward* neologism has been introduced, by which the *present passive participle* is substituted, in such cases as the above, for the participle in *ing*."—*Ibid.* He has two instances more, in each of which the phrase is linked with an expression of disapprobation; "' It [[Greek: tetymmenos]] signifies properly, though *in uncouth English,* one who *is being beaten.*' ABP. WHATELY.—'The bridge *is being built,* and other phrases of the like kind, *have* pained the eye.' D. BOOTH."—*Ibid.*[272]

OBS. 24.—Richard Hiley, in the third edition of his Grammar, published in London, in 1840, after showing the passive use of the participle in *ing,* proceeds thus: "No ambiguity arises, we presume, from the use of the participle in this manner. To avoid, however, affixing a passive signification to the participle in *ing,* an attempt has lately been made to substitute the passive participle in its place. Thus instead of 'The house was *building,*' 'The work *imprinting,*' we sometimes hear, 'The house was *being built,*' 'The work is *being printed.*' But this mode is *contrary to the English idiom,* and has not yet obtained the sanction of reputable authority."—*Hiley's Gram.,* p. 30.

OBS. 25.—Professor Hart, of Philadelphia, whose English Grammar was first published in 1845, justly prefers the usage which takes the progressive form occasionally in a passive sense; but, in arguing against the new substitute, he evidently remoulds the early reasoning of Dr. Bullions, errors and all; a part of which he introduces thus: "I know the correctness of this mode of expression has lately been very much assailed, and an attempt, to some extent successful, has been made [,] to introduce the form [,] *'is being built.'* But, in the first place, the old mode of expression is a well established usage of the language, being found in our best and most correct writers. Secondly, *is being built* does not convey the idea intended, [;] namely [,] that of *progressive action. Is being,* taken together, means simply *is,* just as *is writing* means *writes*; therefore, *is being built* means *is built,* a perfect and not a progressive ACTION. Or, if *being* [and] *built* be taken together, *they signify an* ACTION COMPLETE, and the phrase means, as before, *the house is* (EXISTS) *being built.*"—*Hart's Gram.,* p. 76. The last three sentences here are liable to many objections, some of which are suggested above.

OBS. 26.—It is important, that the central phraseology of our language be so understood, as not to be *misinterpreted with credit*, or falsely expounded by popular critics and teachers. Hence errors of *exposition* are the more particularly noticed in these observations. In "*being built*," Prof. Hart, like sundry authors named above, finds nothing but "ACTION COMPLETE." Without doubt, Butler interprets better, when he says, "'The house *is built*,' denotes an *existing state*, rather than a *completed action*." But this author, too, in his next three sentences, utters as many errors; for he adds: "The name of the agent *cannot be expressed* in phrases of this kind. We *cannot say*, 'The house is built *by John*.' When we say, 'The house is built by mechanics,' we *do not express an existing state*."—*Butler's Practical Gram.*, p. 80. Unquestionably, "*is built by mechanics*," expresses *nothing else* than the "*existing state*" of being "built by mechanics," together with an affirmation:—that is, the "existing state" of receiving the action of mechanics, is affirmed of "the house." And, in my judgement, one may very well say, "*The house is built by John*;" meaning, "*John is building the house*." St. Paul says, "Every house *is builded by* SOME MAN."—*Heb.*, iii, 4. In this text, the common "name of the agent" is "expressed."

OBS. 27.—Wells and Weld, whose grammars date from 1846, being remarkably chary of finding anything wrong in "respectable writers," hazard no opinion of their own, concerning the correctness or incorrectness of either of the usages under discussion. They do not always see absurdity in the approbation of opposites; yet one should here, perhaps, count them with the majorities they allow. The latter says, "The participle in *ing* is sometimes used passively; as, forty and six years was this temple in *building*; not in *being built*."—*Weld's English Gram.*, 2d Ed., p. 170. Here, if he means to suggest, that "*in being built*" would "not" be good English, he teaches very erroneously; if his thought is, that this phrase would "not" express the sense of the former one, "*in building,*" he palpably contradicts his own position! But he proceeds, in a note, thus: "The form of expression, *is being built, is being committed,* &c., is almost universally condemned by grammarians; but it is *sometimes* met with in respectable writers. It occurs most frequently in newspaper paragraphs, and in hasty compositions."—*Ibid.* Wells comments thus: "Different opinions have long existed among critics respecting this passive use of the imperfect participle. Many respectable writers substitute the compound passive participle; as, 'The house is *being built*;' 'The book is *being printed*.' But the prevailing practice of the best authors is in favor of the *simple form*; as, 'The house *is building*.'"—*Wells's School Gram.,* 1st Ed., p. 148; 113th Ed., p. 161.[273]

OBS. 28.—S. W. Clark, in the second edition of his Practical Grammar, stereotyped and published in New York in 1848, appears to favour the insertion of "*being*" into passive verbs; but his instructions are so obscure, so often inaccurate, and so incompatible one with an other, that it is hard to say, with certainty, what he approves. In one place, he has this position: "The Passive Voice of a verb is formed by adding the *Passive Participle* of that verb, to the verb *be*. EXAMPLES—To *be* loved. I *am* feared. They *are* worshipped."—Page 69. In an other, he has this: "When the Subject is to be represented as receiving the action, *the Passive Participle* should be used. EXAMPLE—Henry's *lesson* is BEING RECITED."—P. 132. Now these two positions utterly confound each other; for they are equally general, and "*the Passive Participle*" is first one thing, and then an other. Again, he has the following assertions, both false: "The Present (or First) Participle *always* ends in *ing,* and is *limited to the Active Voice.* The Past (or Second) Participle of Regular Verbs ends in *d* or *ed,* and is *limited to the Passive Voice.*"—P. 131. Afterwards, in spite of the fancied limitation, he acknowledges the passive use of the participle in *ing,* and that there is "*authority*" for it; but, at the same time, most absurdly supposes the word to predicate "*action*," and also to be *wrong*: saying, "*Action* is *sometimes* predicated of a *passive* subject. EXAMPLE—'The *house is building*,.. for.. 'The *house is being built*,'.. which means.. The house *is becoming built*." On this, he remarks thus: "This is one of the instances in which *Authority* is against *Philosophy*. For an *act* cannot *properly* be predicated of a *passive agent*. Many good writers *properly reject* this idiom. 'Mansfield's prophecy *is being realized*.'—MICHELET'S LUTHER."—*Clark's Practical Gram.*, p. 133. It may require some study to learn from this *which idiom it is*. that these "many good writers reject:" but the grammarian who can talk of "*a passive agent*," without perceiving that the phrase is self-contradictory and absurd, may well be expected to entertain a "Philosophy" which is against "Authority," and likewise to prefer a ridiculous innovation to good and established usage.

OBS. 29.—As most verbs are susceptible of both forms, the simple active and the compound or progressive, and likewise of a transitive and an intransitive sense in each; and as many, when taken intransitively, may have a meaning which is scarcely distinguishable from that of the passive form; it often happens that this substitution of the imperfect participle passive for the simple imperfect in *ing*, is quite needless, even when the latter is not considered passive. For example: "See by the following paragraph, how widely the bane *is being circulated*!"—*Liberator*, No. 999, p. 34. Here *is circulating* would be better; and so would *is circulated*. Nor would either of these much vary the sense, if at all; for "*circulate*" may mean, according to Webster, "*to be diffused*," or, as Johnson and Worcester have it, "*to be dispersed*." See the second marginal note on p. 378.

OBS. 30.—R. G. Parker appears to have formed a just opinion of the "modern innovation," the arguments for which are so largely examined in the foregoing observations; but the "principle" which he adduces as "conclusive" against it, if *principle* it can be called, has scarcely any bearing on the question; certainly no more than has the simple assertion of one reputable critic, that our participle in *ing* may occasionally be used passively. "Such expressions as the following," says he, "have recently become very common, not only in the periodical publications of the day, but are likewise finding favor with popular writers; as, 'The house *is being built*.' 'The street *is being paved*.' 'The actions that *are* now *being performed*,' &c. 'The patents *are being prepared*.' The usage of the best writers does not sanction these expressions; and Mr. Pickbourn lays down the following principle, which is conclusive upon the subject. '*Whenever the participle* in *ing* is joined by an auxiliary verb to a nominative capable of the action, it is taken actively; but, when joined to one incapable of the action, it becomes passive. If we say, *The man are building a house*, the participle *building* is evidently used in an active sense; *because* the men are capable of the action. But when we say, *The house is building*, or, *Patents are preparing*, the participles *building* and *preparing* must necessarily be understood in a passive sense; because neither the house nor the patents are capable of action.'—See Pickbourn on the English Verb, pp. 78-80."—*Parker's Aids to English Composition*, p. 105. Pickbourn wrote his Dissertation before the question arose which he is here supposed to decide. Nor is he right in assuming that the common Progressive Form, of which he speaks, must be either *active-transitive* or *passive*: I have shown above that it may be *active-intransitive,* and perhaps, in a few instances, *neuter*. The class of the verb is determined by something else than the mere *capableness* of the "*nominative*."


## III. FORM OF PASSIVE VERBS.

Passive verbs, in English, are always of a compound form; being made from active-transitive verbs, by adding the Perfect Participle to the auxiliary verb BE, through all its changes: thus from the active-transitive verb *love*, is formed the passive verb *be loved*.

## FIFTH EXAMPLE.

The regular passive verb BE LOVED, conjugated affirmatively.

PRINCIPAL PARTS or THE ACTIVE VERB.

*Present. Preterit. Imp. Participle. Perf. Participle.*

Love. Loved. Loving. Loved.

INFINITIVE MOOD.
PRESENT TENSE.
To be loved.

PERFECT TENSE.
To have been loved.

### INDICATIVE MOOD.

PRESENT TENSE. *Singular. Plural.* 1. I am loved, 1. We are loved, 2. Thou art loved, 2. You are loved, 3. He is loved; 3. They are loved.

IMPERFECT TENSE. *Singular. Plural.* 1. I was loved, 1. We were loved, 2. Thou wast loved, 2. You were loved, 3. He was loved; 3. They were loved.

PERFECT TENSE. *Singular. Plural.* 1. I have been loved, 1. We have been loved, 2. Thou hast been loved, 2. You have been loved, 3. He has been loved; 3. They have been loved.

PLUPERFECT TENSE. *Singular*. *Plural*. 1. I had been loved, 1. We had been loved, 2. Thou hadst been loved, 2. You had been loved, 3. He had been loved; 3. They had been loved.

FIRST-FUTURE TENSE. *Singular*. *Plural*. 1. I shall be loved, 1. We shall be loved, 2. Thou wilt be loved, 2. You will be loved, 3. He will be loved; 3. They will be loved.

SECOND-FUTURE TENSE. *Singular*. *Plural*. 1. I shall have been loved, 1. We shall have been loved, 2. Thou wilt have been loved, 2. You will have been loved, 3. He will have been loved; 3. They will have been loved.

**POTENTIAL MOOD.**

PRESENT TENSE. *Singular*. *Plural*. 1. I may be loved, 1. We may be loved, 2. Thou mayst be loved, 2. You may be loved, 3. He may be loved; 3. They may be loved.

IMPERFECT TENSE. *Singular*. *Plural*. 1. I might be loved, 1. We might be loved, 2. Thou mightst be loved, 2. You might be loved, 3. He might be loved; 3. They might be loved.

PERFECT TENSE. *Singular*. *Plural*. 1. I may have been loved, 1. We may have been loved, 2. Thou mayst have been loved, 2. You may have been loved, 3. He may have been loved; 3. They may have been loved.

**PLUPERFECT TENSE.**

*Singular*. *Plural*. 1. I might have been loved, 1. We might have been loved, 2. Thou mightst have been loved, 2. You might have been loved, 3. He might have been loved; 3. They might have been loved.

**SUBJUNCTIVE MOOD.**

**PRESENT TENSE.**

*Singular*. *Plural*. 1. If I be loved, 1. If we be loved, 2. If thou be loved, 2. If you be loved, 3. If he be loved; 3. If they be loved.

**IMPERFECT TENSE.**

*Singular*. *Plural*. 1. If I were loved, 1. If we were loved, 2. If thou were loved, 2. If you were loved, 3. If he were loved; 3. If they were loved.

**IMPERATIVE MOOD.**

**PRESENT TENSE.**

*Singular*. 2. Be [thou] loved, *or* Do thou be loved; *Plural*. 2. Be [ye or you] loved, *or* Do you be loved.

**PARTICIPLES.**

1. *The Imperfect*. 2. *The Perfect*. 3. *The Preperfect*. Being loved. Loved. Having been loved.

FAMILIAR FORM WITH 'THOU.' NOTE.—In the familiar style, the second person singular of this verb, is usually and more properly formed thus: IND. Thou art loved, Thou was loved, Thou hast been loved, Thou had been loved, Thou shall or will be loved, Thou shall or will have been loved. POT. Thou may, can, *or* must be loved; Thou might, could, would, *or* should be loved; Thou may, can, *or* must have been loved; Thou might, could, would, *or* should have been loved. SUBJ. If thou be loved, If thou were loved. IMP. Be [thou] loved, or Do thou be loved.

# OBSERVATIONS.

OBS. 1.—A few active-intransitive verbs, that signify mere motion, change of place, or change of condition, may be put into this form, with a *neuter* signification; making not *passive* but *neuter* verbs, which express nothing more than the state which results from the change: as, "*I am come.*"—"*She is gone.*"—"*He is risen.*"—"*They are fallen.*" These are what Dr. Johnson and some others call "*neuter* passives;" a name which never was very proper, and for which we have no frequent use.

OBS. 2.—Most neuter verbs of the passive form, such as, "*am grown, art become, is lain, are flown, are vanished, are departed, was sat, were arrived,*" may now be considered errors of conjugation, or perhaps of syntax. In the verb, *to be mistaken,* there is an irregularity which ought to be particularly noticed. When applied to *persons,* this verb is commonly taken in a *neuter* sense, and signifies, *to be in error, to be wrong*; as, "I *am mistaken,* thou *art mistaken,* he *is mistake.*" But, when used of *things,* it is a proper passive verb, and signifies, *to be misunderstood,* or *to be taken wrong*; as, "The sense of the passage *is mistaken*; that is, not rightly understood." See *Webster's Dict., w. Mistaken.* "I have known a shadow across a brook *to be mistaken* for a footbridge."

OBS. 3.—Passive verbs may be easily distinguished from neuter verbs of the same form, by a reference to the agent or instrument, common to the former class, but not to the latter. This frequently is, and always may be, expressed after *passive* verbs; but never is, and never can be, expressed after *neuter* verbs: as, "The thief has been caught *by the officer.*"— "Pens are made *with a knife.*" Here the verbs are passive; but, "*I am not yet ascended,*" (John, xx, 17,) is not passive, because it does not convey the idea of being ascended *by* some one's agency.

OBS. 4.—Our ancient writers, after the manner of the French, very frequently employed this mode of conjugation in a neuter sense; but, with a very few exceptions, present usage is clearly in favour of the auxiliary *have* in preference to *be*, whenever the verb formed with the perfect participle is not passive; as, "They *have* arrived,"—not, "They *are* arrived." Hence such examples as the following, are not now good English: "All these reasons *are* now ceased."—*Butler's Analogy*, p. 157. Say, "*have now* ceased." "Whether he *were* not got beyond the reach of his faculties."—*Ib.*, p. 158. Say, "*had* not got." "Which *is* now grown wholly obsolete."—*Churchill's Gram.*, p. 330. Say, "*has* now grown." "And when he *was* entered into a ship."—*Bible*. Say, "*had* entered."— "What *is* become of decency and virtue?"—*Murray's Key*, p. 196. Say, "*has* become."

OBS. 5.—Dr. Priestley says, "It seems *not to have been determined* by the English grammarians, whether the *passive* participles of verbs neuter require the auxiliary *am* or *have* before them. The French, in this case, confine themselves strictly to the former. 'What *has become* of national liberty?' Hume's History, Vol. 6. p. 254. The French would say, *what is become*; and, in this instance, perhaps, with more propriety."— *Priestley's Gram.*, p. 128. It is no marvel that those writers who have not rightly made up their minds upon this point of English grammar, should consequently fall into many mistakes. The perfect participle of a neuter verb is not "*passive*," as the doctor seems to suppose it to be; and the mode of conjugation which he here inclines to prefer, is a mere *Gallicism*, which is fast wearing out from our language, and is even now but little countenanced by good writers.

OBS. 6.—There are a few verbs of the passive form which seem to imply that a person's own mind is the agent that actuates him; as, "The editor *is rejoiced* to think," &c.—*Juvenile Keepsake*. "I *am resolved* what to do."— *Luke*, xvi, 4. "He *was resolved* on going to the city to reside."—*Comly's Gram.*, p. 114. "James *was resolved* not to indulge himself."—*Murray's Key*, ii, 220. "He *is inclined* to go."—"He *is determined* to go."—"He *is bent* on going." These are properly passive verbs, notwithstanding there are active forms which are nearly equivalent to most of them; as, "The editor *rejoices* to think."—"I *know* what to do."—"He *had resolved* on going."—"James *resolved* not to indulge himself." So in the phrase, "I *am ashamed* to beg," we seem to have a passive verb of this sort; but, the verb *to ashame* being now obsolete, *ashamed* is commonly reckoned an *adjective*. Yet we cannot put it before a noun, after the usual manner of adjectives. *To be indebted*, is an other expression of the same kind. In the following example, "*am remember'd*" is used for *do remember*, and, in my opinion, *inaccurately*:

> "He said mine eyes were black, and my hair black;
> And, now I *am remember'd*, scorn'd at me."—*Shakspeare.*

## IV. FORM OF NEGATION.

A verb is conjugated *negatively*, by placing the adverb *not* after it, or after the first auxiliary; but the infinitive and participles take the negative first: as, Not to love, Not to have loved; Not loving, Not loved, Not having loved.

**FIRST PERSON SINGULAR.**

IND. I love not, *or* I do not love; I loved not, *or* I did not love; I have not loved; I had not loved; I shall not, *or* will not, love; I shall not, *or* will not, have loved. POT. I may, can, *or* must not love; I might, could, would, *or* should not love; I may, can, *or* must not have loved; I might, could, would, *or* should not have loved, SUBJ. If I love not, If I loved not.

**SECOND PERSON SINGULAR.**

SOLEMN STYLE:—IND. Thou lovest not, *or* Thou dost not love; Thou lovedst not, *or* Thou didst not love; Thou hast not loved; Thou hadst not loved; Thou shalt not, *or* wilt not, love; Thou shalt not, *or* wilt not, have loved. POT. Thou mayst, canst, *or* must not love; Thou mightst, couldst, wouldst, *or* shouldst not love; Thou mayst, canst, *or* must not have loved; Thou mightst, couldst, wouldst, *or* shouldst not have loved. SUBJ. If thou love not, If thou loved not. IMP. Love [thou] not, *or* Do thou not love.

FAMILIAR STYLE:—IND. Thou lov'st not, *or* Thou dost not love; Thou loved not, *or* Thou did not love; Thou hast not loved; Thou had not loved; Thou shall not, *or* will not, love; Thou shall not, *or* will not, have loved. POT. Thou may, can, *or* must not love; Thou might, could, would, *or* should not love; Thou may, can, *or* must not have loved; Thou might, could, would, *or* should not have loved. SUBJ. If thou love not, If thou loved not. IMP. Love [thou] not, *or* Do [thou] not love.

**THIRD PERSON SINGULAR.**

IND. He loves not, *or* He does not love; He loved not, *or* He did not love; He has not loved; He had not loved; He shall not, *or* will not, love; He shall not, *or* will not, have loved. POT. He may, can, *or* must not love; He might, could, would, *or* should not love; He may, can, *or* must not have loved; He might, could, would, *or* should not have loved. SUBJ. If he love not, If he loved not.

**V. FORM OF QUESTION.**

A verb is conjugated *interrogatively*, in the indicative and potential moods, by placing the nominative after it, or after the first auxiliary: as,

**FIRST PERSON SINGULAR.**

IND. Love I? *or* Do I love? Loved I? *or* Did I love? Have I loved? Had I loved? Shall I love? Shall I have loved? POT. May, can, *or* must I love?

Might, could, would, *or* should I love? May, can, *or* must I have loved? Might, could, would, *or* should I have loved?

**SECOND PERSON SINGULAR.**

SOLEMN STYLE:—IND. Lovest thou? *or* Dost thou love? Lovedst thou? *or* Didst thou love? Hast thou loved? Hadst thou loved? Wilt thou love? Wilt thou have loved? POT. Mayst, canst, *or* must thou love? Mightst, couldst, wouldst, *or* shouldst thou love? Mayst, canst, *or* must thou have loved? Mightst, couldst, wouldst, *or* shouldst thou have loved?

FAMILIAR STYLE:—IND. Lov'st thou? *or* Dost thou love? Loved thou? *or* Did thou love? Hast thou loved? Had thou loved? Will thou love? Will thou have loved? POT. May, can, *or* must thou love? Might, could, would, *or* should thou love? May, can, *or* must thou have loved? Might, could, would, *or* should thou have loved?

**THIRD PERSON SINGULAR.**

IND. Loves he? *or* Does he love? Loved he? *or* Did he love? Has he loved? Had he loved? Shall *or* will he love? Will he have loved? POT. May, can, *or* must he love? Might, could, would, *or* should he love? May, can, *or* must he have loved? Might, could, would, *or* should he have loved?

**VI. FORM OF QUESTION WITH NEGATION.**

A verb is conjugated *interrogatively and negatively*, in the indicative and potential moods, by placing the nominative and the adverb *not* after the verb, or after the first auxiliary: as,

**FIRST PERSON PLURAL.**

IND. Love we not? *or* Do we not love? Loved we not? *or* Did we not love? Have we not loved? Had we not loved? Shall we not love? Shall we not have loved? POT. May, can, *or* must we not love? Might, could, would, *or* should we not love? May, can, *or* must we not have loved? Might, could, would, *or* should we not have loved?

**SECOND PERSON PLURAL.**

IND. See ye not? *or* Do you not see? Saw ye not? *or* Did you not see? Have you not seen? Had you not seen? Will you not see? Will you not have seen? POT. May, can, *or* must you not see? Might, could, would, *or* should you not see? May, can, *or* must you not have seen? Might, could, would, *or* should you not have seen?

**THIRD PERSON PLURAL.**

IND. Are they not loved? Were they not loved? Have they not been loved? Had they not been loved? Shall *or* will they not be loved? Will they not have been loved? May, can, *or* must they not be loved? Might, could, would, *or* should they not be loved? May, can, *or* must they not have been loved? Might, could, would, *or* should they not have been loved?

## OBSERVATIONS.

OBS. 1.—In a familiar question or negation, the compound or auxiliary form of the verb is, in general, preferable to the simple: as, "No man lives to purpose, who *does not live* for posterity."—*Dr. Wayland.* It is indeed so much more common, as to seem the only proper mode of expression: as, "*Do I say* these things as a man?"—"*Do you think* that we excuse ourselves?"—"*Do you not know* that a little leaven *leavens* the whole lump?"—"*Dost thou revile?*" &c. But in the solemn or the poetic style, though either may be used, the simple form is more dignified, and perhaps more graceful: as, "*Say I* these things as a man?"—*1 Cor.*, ix, 8. "*Think ye* that we excuse ourselves?"—*2 Cor.*, xii, 19. "*Know ye not* that a little leaven *leaveneth* the whole lump?"—*1 Cor.*, v, 6. "*Revilest thou* God's high priest?"—*Acts.* "King Agrippa, *believest thou* the prophets?"—*Ib.* "*Understandest thou* what thou readest?"—*Ib.* "Of whom *speaketh* the prophet this?"—*Id.* "And the man of God said, Where *fell it?*"—*2 Kings*, vi, 6.

"What! *heard ye not* of lowland war?"—*Sir W. Scott, L. L.*

"*Seems he not*, Malise, like a ghost?"—*Id., L. of Lake.*

"Where *thinkst thou* he is now? *Stands he*, or *sits he?*
Or *does he walk?* or *is he* on his horse?"—*Shak., Ant. and Cleop.*

OBS. 2.—In interrogative sentences, the auxiliaries *shall* and *will* are not always capable of being applied to the different persons agreeably to their use in simple declarations: thus, "*Will* I go?" is a question which there never can be any occasion to ask in its literal sense; because none knows better than I, what my will or wish is. But "*Shall* I go?" may properly be asked; because *shall* here refers to *duty*, and asks to know what is agreeable to the will of an other. In questions, the first person generally requires *shall*; the second, *will*; the third admits of both: but, in the second-future, the third, used interrogatively, seems to require *will* only. Yet, in that figurative kind of interrogation which is sometimes used to declare a negative, there may be occasional exceptions to these principles; as, "*Will I eat* the flesh of bulls, or drink the blood of goats?"—*Psalms*, 1, 13. That is, *I will not eat,* &c.

OBS. 3.—*Cannot* is not properly one word, but two: in parsing, the adverb must be taken separately, and the auxiliary be explained with its principal. When power is denied, *can* and *not* are now *generally united*—perhaps in order to prevent ambiguity; as, "I *cannot* go." But when the power is affirmed, and something else is denied, the words are written separately; as, "The Christian apologist *can not merely* expose the utter baseness of the infidel assertion, but he has positive ground for erecting an opposite and confronting assertion in its place."—*Dr. Chalmers.* The junction of these terms, however, is not of much importance to the sense; and, as it is plainly contrary to analogy, some writers,—(as Dr. Webster, in his late or "improved" works; Dr. Bullions, in his; Prof. W. C. Fowler, in his new "English Grammar," 8vo; R. C. Trench, in his "Study of Words;" T. S. Pinneo, in his "revised" grammars; J. R. Chandler, W. S. Cardell, O. B. Peirce,—) always separate them. And, indeed, why should we write, "I *cannot* go, Thou *canst not* go, He *cannot* go?" Apart from the custom, we have just as good reason to join *not* to *canst* as to *can*; and sometimes its union with the latter is a gross error: as, "He *cannot only* make a way to escape, but with the injunction to duty can infuse the power to perform."—*Maturin's Sermons*, p. 287. The fear of ambiguity never prevents us from disjoining *can* and *not* whenever we wish to put a word between them: as, "Though the waves thereof toss themselves, yet *can* they *not* prevail; though they roar, yet *can* they *not* pass over it."—*Jeremiah*, v, 22. "Which then I *can* resist *not*."—*Byron's Manfred*, p. 1.

"*Can* I *not* mountain maiden spy, But she must bear the Douglas eye?"—*Scott.*

OBS. 4.—In negative questions, the adverb *not* is sometimes placed before the nominative, and sometimes after it: as, "Told *not I* thee?"—*Numb.*, xxiii, 26. "Spake *I not* also to thy messengers?"—*Ib.*, xxiv, 12. "*Cannot I* do with you as this potter?"—*Jer.*, xviii, 6. "Art *not thou* a seer?"—*2 Sam.*, xv, 27. "Did *not Israel* know?"—*Rom.*, x, 19. "Have *they not* heard?"—*Ib.*, 18. "Do *not they* blaspheme that worthy name?"—*James,* ii, 7. This adverb, like every other, should be placed where it will sound most agreeably, and best suit the sense. Dr. Priestley imagined that it could not properly come before the nominative. He says, "When the nominative case is put after the verb, on account of *an* interrogation, *no other word* should be interposed between them. [EXAMPLES:] 'May *not we* here say with Lucretius?'—Addison on Medals, p. 29. May *we not* say? 'Is *not it* he.' [?] Smollett's Voltaire, Vol 18, p. 152. Is *it not* he. [?]"—*Priestley's Gram.*, p. 177.

OBS. 5.—In grave discourse, or in oratory, the adverb *not* is spoken as distinctly as other words; but, *ordinarily,* when placed before the nominative, it is rapidly slurred over in utterance and the *o* is not heard. In fact, it is *generally* (though inelegantly) contracted in familiar conversation, and joined to the auxiliary: as, IND. Don't they do it? Didn't they do it? Haven't they done it? Hadn't they done it? Shan't, *or* won't they do it? Won't they have done it? POT. Mayn't, can't, *or* mustn't they do it? Mightn't, couldn't, wouldn't, *or* shouldn't they do it? Mayn't, can't, *or* mustn't they have done it? Mightn't, couldn't, wouldn't, *or* shouldn't they have done it?

OBS. 6.—Well-educated people commonly utter their words with more distinctness and fullness than the vulgar, yet without adopting ordinarily the long-drawn syllables of poets and orators, or the solemn phraseology of preachers and prophets. Whatever may be thought of the grammatical propriety of such contractions as the foregoing, no one who has ever observed how the English language is usually spoken, will doubt their commonness, or their antiquity. And it may be observed, that, in the use of these forms, the distinction of persons and numbers in the verb, is almost, if not entirely, dropped. Thus *don't* is used for *dost not* or *does not,* as properly as for *do not*; and, "*Thou can't* do it, or *shan't* do it," is as good English as, "*He can't* do it, or *shan't* do it." *Will,* according to Webster, was anciently written *woll*: hence *won't* acquired the *o*, which is long in Walker's orthoëpy. *Haven't,* which cannot be used for *has not* or *hast not,* is still further contracted by the vulgar, and spoken *ha'nt,* which serves for all three. These forms are sometimes found in books; as, "WONT, a contraction of *woll not,* that is, *will not."—Webster's Dict.* "HA'NT, a contraction of *have not* or *has not."—Id.* "WONT, (w=ont *or* w~unt,) A contraction of *would not*:— used for *will* not."—*Worcester's Dict.* "HAN'T, (hänt or h=ant,) A vulgar contraction for *has not,* or *have not."—Id.* In the writing of such contractions, the apostrophe is not always used; though some think it necessary for distinction's sake: as, "Which is equivalent, because what *can't* be done *won't* be done."—*Johnson's Gram. Com.,* p. 312.

# IRREGULAR VERBS.

An *irregular verb* is a verb that does not form the preterit and the perfect participle by assuming *d* or *ed*; as, *see, saw, seeing, seen*. Of this class of verbs there are about one hundred and ten, beside their several derivatives and compounds.

## OBSERVATIONS.

OBS. 1.—Regular verbs form their preterits and perfect participles, by adding *d* to final *e*, and *ed* to all other terminations; the final consonant of the verb being sometimes doubled, (as in *dropped*,) and final *y* sometimes changed into *i*, (as in *cried*,) agreeably to the rules for spelling in such cases. The verb *hear, heard, hearing, heard*, adds *d* to *r*, and is therefore irregular. *Heard* is pronounced *h~erd* by all our lexicographers, except *Webster*: who formerly wrote it *heerd*, and still pronounces it so; alleging, in despite of universal usage against him, that it is written "more correctly *heared*."—*Octavo Dict.*, 1829. Such pronunciation would doubtless require this last orthography, "*heared*;" but both are, in fact, about as fanciful as his former mode of spelling, which ran thus: "*Az* I had *heerd* suggested by *frends* or indifferent *reeders*."—*Dr. Webster's Essays, Preface*, p. 10.

OBS. 2.—When a verb ends in a sharp consonant, *t* is sometimes improperly substituted for *ed*, making the preterit and the perfect participle irregular in spelling, when they are not so in sound; as, *distrest* for *distressed, tost* for *tossed, mixt* for *mixed, cract* for *cracked*. These contractions are now generally treated as *errors* in writing; and the verbs are accordingly (with a few exceptions) accounted regular. Lord Kames commends Dean Swift for having done "all in his power to restore the syllable *ed*;" says, he "possessed, if any man ever did, the true genius of the English tongue;" and thinks that in rejecting these ugly contractions, "he well deserves to be imitated."—*Elements of Criticism*, Vol. ii, p. 12. The regular orthography is indeed to be preferred in all such cases; but the writing of *ed* restores no syllable, except in solemn discourse; and, after all, the poems of Swift have so very many of these irregular contractions in *t*, that one can hardly believe his lordship had ever read them. Since the days of these critics still more has been done towards the restoration of the *ed*, in orthography, though not in sound; but, even at this present time, our poets not unfrequently write, *est* for *essed* or *ess'd*, in forming the preterits or participles of verbs that end in the syllable *ess*. This is an ill practice, which needlessly multiplies our redundant verbs, and greatly embarrasses what it seems at first to simplify: as,

"O friend! I know not which way I must look
For comfort, being, as I am, *opprest*,
To think that now our life is only *drest*
For show."—*Wordsworth's Poetical Works*, 8vo, p. 119.

OBS. 3.—When the verb ends with a smooth consonant, the substitution of *t* for *ed* produces an irregularity in sound as well as in writing. In some such irregularities, the poets are indulged for the sake of rhyme; but the best speakers and writers of prose prefer the regular form, wherever good use has sanctioned it: thus *learned* is better than *learnt; burned*, than *burnt; penned*, than *pent; absorbed*, than *absorbt; spelled*, than *spelt; smelled*, than *smelt*. So many of this sort of words as are allowably contracted, belong to the class of redundant verbs, among which they may be seen in a subsequent table.

OBS. 4.—Several of the irregular verbs are variously used by the best authors; redundant forms are occasionally given to some verbs, without sufficient authority; and many preterits and participles which were formerly in good use, are now obsolete, or becoming so. The *simple* irregular verbs in English are about one hundred and ten, and they are nearly all monosyllables. They are derived from the Saxon, in which language they are also, for the most part, irregular.

OBS. 5.—The following alphabetical list exhibits the simple irregular verbs, as they are *now generally* used. In this list, those preterits and participles which are supposed to be preferable, and best supported by authorities, are placed first. Nearly all compounds that follow the form of their simple verbs, or derivatives that follow their primitives, are here purposely omitted. *Welcome* and *behave* are always regular, and therefore belong not here. Some words which are obsolete, have also been omitted, that the learner might not mistake them for words in present use. Some of those which are placed last, are now little used.

**LIST OF THE IRREGULAR VERBS.**

|  |  | *Imperfect* | *Perfect* |
| --- | --- | --- | --- |
| *Present.* | *Preterit.* | *Participle.* | *Participle.* |

Arise, arose, arising, arisen.
Be, was, being, been.
Bear, bore *or* bare, bearing, borne *or* born.[274]
Beat, beat, beating, beaten *or* beat.
Begin, began *or* begun,[275] beginning, begun.
Behold, beheld, beholding, beheld.
Beset, beset, besetting, beset.
Bestead, bestead, besteading, bestead.[276]

Bid, bid *or* bade, bidding, bidden *or* bid.

Bind, bound, bing, bound.

Bite, bit, biting, bitten *or* bit.

Bleed, bled, bleeding, bled.

Break, broke,[277] breaking, broken.

Breed, bred, breeding, bred.

Bring, brought, bringing, brought.

Buy, bought, buying, bought.

Cast, cast, casting, cast.

Chide, chid, chiding, chidden *or* chid.

Choose, chose, choosing, chosen.

Cleave,[278] cleft *or* clove, cleaving, cleft *or* cloven.

Cling, clung, clinging, clung.

Come, came, coming, come.

Cost, cost, costing, cost.

Cut, cut, cutting, cut.

Do, did, doing, done.

Draw, drew, drawing, drawn.

Drink, drank, drinking, drunk, *or* drank.[279]

Drive, drove, driving, driven.

Eat, ate *or* ~eat, eating, eaten *or* eat.

Fall, fell, falling, fallen.

Feed, fed, feeding, fed.

Feel, felt, feeling, felt.

Fight, fought, fighting, fought.

Find, found, finding, found.

Flee, fled, fleeing, fled.

Fling, flung, flinging, flung.

Fly, flew, flying, flown.

Forbear, forbore, forbearing, forborne.

Forsake, forsook, forsaking, forsaken.

Get, got, getting, got *or* gotten.

Give, gave, giving, given.

Go, went, going, gone.

Grow, grew, growing, grown.

Have, had, having, had.

Hear, heard, hearing, heard.

Hide, hid, hiding, hidden *or* hid.

Hit, hit, hitting, hit.

Hold, held, holding, held *or* holden.[280]

Hurt, hurt, hurting, hurt.[281]

Keep, kept,[282] keeping, kept.

Know, knew, knowing, known.

Lead, led, leading, led.

Leave, left, leaving, left.

Lend, lent, lending, lent.

Let, let, letting, let

Lie,[283] lay, lying, lain.

Lose, lost, losing, lost.

Make, made, making, made.

Meet, met, meeting, met.

Outdo, outdid, outdoing, outdone.

Put, put, putting, put.

Read, r~ead, reading, r~ead.

Rend, rent, rending, rent.[284]

Rid, rid, ridding, rid.

Ride, rode, riding, ridden *or* rode.

Ring, rung *or* rang, ringing, rung.

Rise, rose, rising, risen.

Run, ran *or* run, running, run.

Say, said, saying, said.[285]

See, saw, seeing, seen.

Seek, sought, seeking, sought.

Sell, sold, selling, sold.

Send, sent, sending, sent.

Set, set, setting, set.

Shed, shed, shedding, shed.

Shoe, shod, shoeing, shod.[286]

Shoot, shot, shooting, shot.

Shut, shut, shutting, shut.

Shred, shred, shredding, shred.

Shrink, shrunk *or* shrank, shrinking, shrunk *or* shrunken.

Sing, sung *or* sang,[287] singing, sung.

Sink, sunk *or* sank, sinking, sunk.

Sit, sat, sitting, sat.[288]

Slay, slew, slaying, slain.

Sling, slung, slinging, slung.

Slink, slunk *or* slank, slinking, slunk.

Smite, smote, smiting, smitten *or* smit.

Speak, spoke, speaking, spoken.

Spend, spent, spending, spent.

Spin, spun, spinning, spun.

Spit, spit *or* spat, spitting, spit *or* spitten.

Spread, spread, spreading, spread.

Spring, sprung *or* sprang, springing, sprung.

Stand, stood, standing, stood.

Steal, stole, stealing, stolen.

Stick, stuck, sticking, stuck.

Sting, stung, stinging, stung.

Stink, stunk *or* stank, stinking, stunk.

Stride, strode *or* strid, striding, stridden

or strid.[289]

Strike, struck, striking, struck *or* stricken.

Swear, swore, swearing, sworn.

Swim, swum *or* swam, swimming, swum.

Swing, swung *or* swang, swinging, swung.

Take, took, taking, taken.

Teach, taught, teaching, taught.

Tear, tore, tearing, torn.

Tell, told, telling, told.

Think, thought, thinking, thought.

Thrust, thrust, thrusting, thrust.

Tread, trod, treading, trodden *or* trod.

Wear, wore, wearing, worn.

Win, won, winning, won.

Write, wrote, writing, written.[290]


## REDUNDANT VERBS.

A *redundant verb* is a verb that forms the preterit or the perfect participle in two or more ways, and so as to be both regular and irregular; as, *thrive, thrived* or *throve, thriving, thrived* or *thriven*. Of this class of verbs, there are about ninety-five, beside sundry derivatives and compounds.


## OBSERVATIONS.

OBS. 1.—Those irregular verbs which have more than one form for the preterit or for the perfect participle, are in some sense redundant; but, as there is no occasion to make a distinct class of such as have double forms that are never regular, these redundancies are either included in the preceding list of the simple irregular verbs, or omitted as being improper to be now recognized for good English. Several examples of the latter kind, including both innovations and archaisms, will appear among the improprieties for correction, at the end of this chapter. A few old preterits or participles may perhaps be accounted good English in the solemn style, which are not so in the familiar: as, "And none *spake* a word unto him."—*Job*, ii, 13. "When I *brake* the five loaves."—*Mark*, viii, 19. "And he *drave* them from the judgement-seat."—*Acts*, xviii, 16. "Serve me till I have eaten and *drunken*."—*Luke*, xvii, 8. "It was not possible that he should be *holden* of it."—*Acts*, ii, 24. "Thou *castedst* them down into destruction."—*Psal.*, lxxiii, 18. "Behold, I was *shapen* in iniquity."—*Ib.*, li, 5. "A meat-offering *baken* in the oven."—*Leviticus*, ii, 4.

"With *casted* slough, and fresh celerity."—SHAK., *Henry V*.

"Thy dreadful vow, *loaden* with death."—ADDISON: *in Joh. Dict.*

OBS. 2.—The verb *bet* is given in Worcester's Dictionary, as being always regular: "BET, *v. a.* [*i.* BETTED; *pp.* BETTING, BETTED.] To wager; to lay a wager or bet. SHAK."—*Octavo Dict.* In Ainsworth's Grammar, it is given as being always irregular: "*Present*, Bet; *Imperfect*, Bet; *Participle*, Bet."—Page 36. On the authority of these, and of some others cited in OBS. 6th below, I have put it with the redundant verbs. The verb *prove* is redundant, if *proven*, which is noticed by Webster, Bolles, and Worcester, is an admissible word. "The participle *proven* is used in Scotland and in some parts of the United States, and sometimes, though rarely, in England.—'There is a mighty difference between *not proven* and *disproven*.' DR. TH. CHALMERS. 'Not *proven*.' QU. REV."—*Worcester's Universal and Critical Dict.* The verbs *bless* and *dress* are to be considered redundant, according to the authority of Worcester, Webster, Bolles, and others. Cobbett will have the verbs, *cast, chide, cling, draw, grow, shred, sling, slink, spring, sting, stride, swim, swing,* and *thrust,* to be always regular; but I find no sufficient authority for allowing to any of them a regular form; and therefore leave them, where they always have been, in the list of simple irregulars. These fourteen verbs are a part of the long list of *seventy* which this author says, "are, by some persons, *erroneously* deemed irregular." Of the following *nine* only, is his assertion true; namely, *dip, help, load, overflow, slip, snow, stamp, strip, whip.* These nine ought always to be formed regularly; for all their irregularities may well be reckoned obsolete. After these deductions from this most erroneous catalogue, there remain forty-five other very common verbs, to be disposed of contrary to this author's instructions. All but two of these I shall place in the list of *redundant* verbs; though for the use of *throwed* I find no written authority but his and William B. Fowle's. The two which I do not consider redundant are *spit* and *strew,* of which it may be proper to take more particular notice.

OBS. 3.—*Spit,* to stab, or to put upon a spit, is regular; as, "I *spitted frogs,* I crushed a heap of emmets."—*Dryden. Spit,* to throw out saliva, is irregular, and most properly formed thus: *spit, spit, spitting, spit.* "*Spat* is obsolete."—*Webster's Dict.* It is used in the Bible; as, "He *spat* on the ground, and made clay of the spittle."—*John,* ix, 6. L. Murray gives this verb thus: "Pres. *Spit*; Imp. *spit, spat*; Perf. Part. *spit, spitten.*" NOTE: "*Spitten* is nearly obsolete."—*Octavo Gram.,* p. 106. Sanborn has it thus: "Pres. *Spit*; Imp. *spit*; Pres. Part. *spitting*; Perf. Part. *spit, spat.*"—*Analytical Gram.,* p. 48. Cobbett, at first, taking it in the form, "to *spit,* I *spat, spitten,*" placed it among the seventy which he so erroneously thought should be made regular; afterwards he left it only in his list of irregulars, thus: "to *spit,* I *spit, spitten.*"—*Cobbett's E. Gram.,* of 1832, p. 54. Churchill, in 1823, preferring the older forms, gave it thus: "*Spit, spat* or *spit, spitten* or *spit.*"— *New Gram.,* p. 111. NOTE:—"Johnson gives *spat* as the preterimperfect, and *spit* or *spitted* as the participle of this verb, when it means to pierce through with a pointed instrument: but in this sense, I believe, it is always regular; while, on the other hand, the regular form is now never used, when it signifies to eject from the mouth; though we find in *Luke*, xviii, 32, 'He shall be *spitted* on.'"—*Churchill's New Gram.*, p. 264. This text ought to have been, "He shall be *spit* upon."

OBS. 4.—*To strew* is in fact nothing else than an other mode of spelling the verb *to strow*; as *shew* is an obsolete form for *show*; but if we pronounce the two forms differently, we make them different words. Walker, and some others, pronounce them alike, *stro*; Sheridan, Jones, Jameson, and Webster, distinguish them in utterance, *stroo* and *stro*. This is convenient for the sake of rhyme, and perhaps therefore preferable. But *strew*, I incline to think, is properly a regular verb only, though Wells and Worcester give it otherwise: if *strewn* has ever been proper, it seems now to be obsolete. EXAMPLES: "Others cut down branches from the trees, and *strewed* them in the way."— *Matt.*, xxi, 8. "Gathering where thou hast not *strewed*."—*Matt.*, xxv, 24.

"Their name, their years, *spelt* by th' unletter'd *muse*,
The place of fame and elegy supply;
And many *a holy text* around she *strews*,
*That teach* the rustic moralist to die."—*Gray.*

OBS. 5.—The list which I give below, prepared with great care, exhibits the redundant verbs, as they are now generally used, or as they may be used without grammatical impropriety.[291] Those forms which are supposed to be preferable, and best supported by authorities, are placed first. No words are inserted here, but such as some modern authors countenance. L. Murray recognizes *bereaved, catched, dealed, digged, dwelled, hanged, knitted, shined, spilled*; and, in his early editions, he approved of *bended, builded, creeped, weaved, worked, wringed*. His two larger books now tell us, "The Compiler *has not inserted* such verbs as *learnt, spelt, spilt*, &c. which are improperly terminated by *t*, instead of *ed*."—*Octavo Gram.*, p. 107;

*Duodecimo*, p. 97. But if he did not, in all his grammars, insert, "*Spill, spilt, R. spilt, R.,*" (pp. 106, 96,) preferring the irregular form to the regular, somebody else has done it for him. And, what is remarkable, many of his *amenders,* as if misled by some evil genius, have contradicted themselves in precisely the same way! Ingersoll, Fisk, Merchant, and Hart, republish exactly the foregoing words, and severally become "*The Compiler*" of the same erroneous catalogue! Kirkham prefers *spilt* to *spilled,* and then declares the word to be "*improperly* terminated by *t* instead of *ed.*"—*Gram.,* p. 151. Greenleaf, who condemns *learnt* and *spelt,* thinks *dwelt* and *spilt* are "the *only established* forms;" yet he will have *dwell* and *spill* to be "*regular*" verbs, as well as "*irregular!*"—*Gram. Simp.,* p. 29. Webber prefers *spilled* to *spilt*; but Picket admits only the latter. Cobbett and Sanborn prefer *bereaved, builded, dealed, digged, dreamed, hanged,* and *knitted,* to *bereft, built, dealt, dug, dreamt, hung,* and *knit.* The former prefers *creeped* to *crept,* and *freezed* to *froze*; the latter, *slitted* to *slit, wringed* to *wrung*; and both consider, "I *bended,*" "I *bursted*" and "I *blowed,*" to be good modern English. W. Allen acknowledges *freezed* and *slided*; and, like Webster, prefers *hove* to *hoven*: but the latter justly prefers *heaved* to both. EXAMP.: "The supple kinsman *slided* to the helm."—*New Timon.* "The rogues *slided* me into the river."—*Shak.* "And the sand *slided* from beneath my feet."— DR. JOHNSON: *in Murray's Sequel,* p. 179. "Wherewith she *freez'd* her foes to congeal'd stone."—*Milton's Comus,* l. 449. "It *freezed* hard last night. Now, what was it that *freezed* so hard?"—*Emmons's Gram.,* p. 25. "Far hence lies, ever *freez'd,* the northern main."—*Savage's Wanderer,* l. 57. "Has he not taught, *beseeched,* and shed abroad the Spirit unconfined?"—*Pollok's Course of Time,* B. x, l. 275.

OBS. 6.—D. Blair supposes *catched* to be an "erroneous" word and unauthorized: "I *catch'd* it," for "I *caught* it," he sets down for a "*vulgarism.*"—*E. Gram.,* p. 111. But *catched* is used by some of the most celebrated authors. Dearborn prefers the regular form of *creep*: "creep, creeped *or* crept, creeped *or* crept."—*Columbian Gram.*, p. 38. I adopt no man's opinions implicitly; copy nothing without examination; but, *to prove all my decisions to be right*, would be an endless task. I shall do as much as ought to be expected, toward showing that they are so. It is to be remembered, that the *poets*, as well as the *vulgar*, use some forms which a *gentleman* would be likely to avoid, unless he meant to quote or imitate; as,

"So *clomb* the first grand thief into God's fold;
So since into his church lewd hirelings climb."
    —*Milton, P. L.*, B. iv, l. 192.

"He *shore* his sheep, and, having packed the wool,
Sent them unguarded to the hill of wolves."
    —*Pollok, C. of T.*, B. vi, l. 306.

————"The King of heav'n
Bar'd his red arm, and launching from the sky
His *writhen* bolt, not shaking empty smoke,
Down to the deep abyss the flaming felon *strook*."
    —*Dryden.*

OBS. 7.—The following are examples in proof of some of the forms acknowledged below: "Where etiquette and precedence *abided* far away."—*Paulding's Westward-Ho!* p. 6. "But there were no secrets where Mrs. Judith Paddock *abided*."—*Ib.*, p. 8. "They *abided* by the forms of government established by the charters."—*John Quincy Adams, Oration*, 1831. "I have *abode* consequences often enough in the course of my life."—*Id., Speech*, 1839. "Present, *bide*, or *abide*; Past, *bode*, or *abode*."—*Coar's Gram.*, p. 104. "I *awaked* up last of all."—*Ecclus.*, xxxiii, 16. "For this are my knees *bended* before the God of the spirits of all flesh."—*Wm. Penn.* "There was never a prince *bereaved* of his dependencies," &c.—*Bacon.* "Madam, you have *bereft* me of all words."—*Shakspeare.* "Reave, *reaved or reft*, reaving, *reaved or reft. Bereave* is similar."—*Ward's Practical Gram.*, p. 65. "And let them tell their tales of woful ages, long ago *betid*."—*Shak.* "Of every nation *blent*, and every age."—*Pollok, C. of T.*, B vii, p. 153. "Rider and horse,—friend, foe,—in one red burial *blent!*"—*Byron, Harold*, C. iii, st. 28. "I *builded* me houses."—*Ecclesiastes*, ii, 4. "For every house is *builded* by some man; but he that *built* all things is God."—*Heb.* iii, 4. "What thy hands *builded* not, thy wisdom gained."—*Milton's P. L.*, X, 373. "Present, *bet*; Past, *bet*; Participle, *bet*."— *Mackintosh's Gram.*, p. 197; *Alexander's*, 38. "John of Gaunt loved him well, and *betted* much upon his head."—SHAKSPEARE: *Joh. Dict, w. Bet.* "He lost every earthly thing he *betted*."—PRIOR: *ib.* "A seraph *kneeled*."—*Pollok, C. T.*, p. 95.

"At first, he declared he himself would be *blowed*,
Ere his conscience with such a foul crime he would load."
—*J. R. Lowell.*

"They are *catched* without art or industry."—*Robertson's Amer.*,-Vol. i, p. 302. "Apt to be *catched* and dazzled."—*Blair's Rhet.*, p. 26. "The lion being *catched* in a net."—*Art of Thinking*, p. 232. "In their self-will they *digged* down a wall."—*Gen.*, xlix, 6. "The royal mother instantly *dove* to the bottom and brought up her babe unharmed."— *Trumbull's America*, i, 144. "The learned have *diven* into the secrets of nature."—CARNOT: *Columbian Orator*, p. 82. "They have *awoke* from that ignorance in which they had slept."—*London Encyclopedia.* "And he *slept* and *dreamed* the second time."—*Gen.*, xli, 5. "So I *awoke*."—*Ib.*, 21. "But he *hanged* the chief baker."—*Gen.*, xl, 22. "Make as if you *hanged* yourself."—ARBUTHNOT: *in Joh. Dict.* "*Graven* by art and man's device."—*Acts*, xvii, 29. "*Grav'd* on the stone beneath yon aged thorn."—*Gray.* "That the tooth of usury may be *grinded*."—*Lord Bacon.* "MILN-EE, The hole from which the *grinded* corn falls into the chest below."—*Glossary of Craven*, London, 1828. "UNGRUND, Not *grinded*."— *Ibid.* "And he *built* the inner court with three rows of *hewed* stone."—*1 Kings*, vi, 36. "A thing by which matter is *hewed*."—*Dr. Murray's Hist. of Europ. Lang.*, Vol. i, p. 378. "SCAGD or SCAD *meaned* distinction, dividing."—*Ib.*, i, 114. "He only *meaned* to acknowledge him to be an extraordinary person."—*Lowth's Gram.*, p. 12. "*The* determines what particular thing is *meaned*."—*Ib.*, p. 11. "If Hermia *mean'd* to say Lysander lied."—*Shak.* "As if I *meaned* not the first but the second creation."—*Barclay's Works*, iii, 289. "From some stones have rivers *bursted* forth."—*Sale's Koran*, Vol. i, p. 14.

"So move we on; I only *meant*
To show the reed on which you *leant*."—*Scott, L. L.*, C. v, st. 11.

OBS. 8.—*Layed*, *payed*, and *stayed*, are now less common than *laid*, *paid*, and *staid*; but perhaps not less correct, since they are the same words in a more regular and not uncommon orthography: "Thou takest up that [which] thou *layedst* not down."—FRIENDS' BIBLE, SMITH'S, BRUCE'S: *Luke*, xix, 21. Scott's Bible, in this place, has "*layest*," which is wrong in tense. "Thou *layedst* affliction upon our loins."—FRIENDS' BIBLE: *Psalms*, lxvi, 11. "Thou *laidest* affliction upon our loins."—SCOTT'S BIBLE, *and* BRUCE'S. "Thou *laidst* affliction upon our loins."—SMITH'S BIBLE, Stereotyped by J. Howe. "Which gently *lay'd* my knighthood on my shoulder."—SINGER'S SHAKSPEARE: *Richard II*, Act i, Sc. 1. "But no regard was *payed* to his remonstrance."—*Smollett's England*, Vol. iii, p. 212. "Therefore the heaven over you is *stayed* from dew, and the earth is *stayed* from her fruit."—*Haggai*, i, 10. "STAY, *i*. STAYED *or* STAID; *pp.* STAYING, STAYED *or* STAID."—*Worcester's Univ. and Crit. Dict.* "Now Jonathan and Ahimaaz *stayed* by En-rogel."—*2 Sam.*, xvii, 17. "This day have I *payed* my vows."—FRIENDS' BIBLE: *Prov*, vii, 14. Scott's Bible has "*paid*." "They not only *stayed* for their resort, but discharged divers."—HAYWARD: *in Joh. Dict.* "I *stayed* till the latest grapes were ripe."—*Waller's Dedication.* "*To lay* is regular, and has in the past time and participle *layed* or *laid*."—*Lowth's Gram.*, p. 54. "To the flood, that *stay'd* her flight."—*Milton's Comus*, l. 832. "All rude, all waste, and desolate is *lay'd*."—*Rowe's Lucan*, B. ix, l. 1636. "And he smote thrice, and *stayed*."—*2 Kings*, xiii, 18.

> "When Cobham, generous as the noble peer
> That wears his honours, *pay'd* the fatal price
> Of virtue blooming, ere the storms were *laid*."—*Shenstone*, p. 167.

OBS. 9.—By the foregoing citations, *lay, pay*, and *stay*, are clearly proved to be redundant. But, in nearly all our English grammars, *lay* and *pay* are represented as being always irregular; and *stay* is as often, and as improperly, supposed to be always regular. Other examples in proof of the list: "I *lit* my pipe with the paper."—*Addison*.

> "While he whom learning, habits, all prevent,
> Is largely *mulct* for each impediment."—*Crabbe, Bor.*, p. 102.
> "And then the chapel—night and morn to pray,
> Or *mulct* and threaten'd if he kept away."—*Ib.*, p. 162.

"A small space is formed, in which the breath is *pent* up."—*Gardiner's Music of Nature*, p. 493. "*Pen*, when it means to write, is always regular. Boyle has *penned* in the sense of confined."—*Churchill's Gram.*, p. 261. "So far as it was now *pled*."—ANDERSON: *Annals of the Bible*, p. 25. "*Rapped* with admiration."—HOOKER: *Joh. Dict.* "And being *rapt* with the love of his beauty."—*Id., ib.* "And *rapt* in secret studies."—SHAK.: *ib.* "I'm *rapt* with joy."—ADDISON: *ib.* "Roast with fire."—FRIENDS' BIBLE: *Exod.*, xii, 8 and 9. "*Roasted* with fire."—SCOTT'S BIBLE: *Exod.*, xii, 8 and 9. "Upon them hath the light *shined*."—*Isaiah*, ix, 2. "The earth *shined* with his glory."—*Ezekiel*, xliii, 2. "After that he had *showed* wonders."—*Acts*, vii, 36. "Those things which God before had *showed*."—*Acts*, iii, 18. "As shall be *shewed* in Syntax."—*Johnson's Gram. Com.*, p.

28. "I have *shown* you, that the *two first* may be dismissed."—*Cobbett's E. Gram.*, ¶ 10. "And in this struggle were *sowed* the seeds of the revolution."—*Everett's Address*, p. 16. "Your favour *showed* to the performance, has given me boldness."—*Jenks's Prayers, Ded.* "Yea, so have I *strived* to preach the gospel."—*Rom.*, xv, 20. "Art thou, like the adder, *waxen* deaf?"—*Shakspeare. "Hamstring'd* behind, unhappy Gyges died."—*Dryden.* "In Syracusa was I born and *wed*."—*Shakspeare.* "And thou art *wedded* to calamity."—*Id.* "I saw thee first, and *wedded* thee."—*Milton.* "Sprung the rank weed, and *thrived* with large increase."—*Pope.* "Some errors never would have *thriven*, had it not been for learned refutation."—*Book of Thoughts*, p. 34. "Under your care they have *thriven*."—*Junius*, p. 5. "Fixed by being rolled closely, compacted, *knitted*."—*Dr. Murray's Hist.*, Vol. i, p. 374. "With kind converse and skill has *weaved*."—*Prior.* "Though I shall be *wetted* to the skin."—*Sandford and Merton*, p. 64. "I *speeded* hither with the very extremest inch of possibility."—*Shakspeare.* "And pure grief *shore* his old thread in twain."—*Id.* "And must I ravel out my *weaved-up* follies?"—*Id., Rich. II.* "Tells how the drudging Goblin *swet*."—*Milton's L'Allegro.* "Weave, wove or *weaved*, weaving, wove, *weaved*, or woven."—*Ward's Gram.*, p. 67.

> "Thou who beneath the frown of fate hast stood,
> And in thy dreadful agony *sweat* blood."—*Young*, p. 238.

OBS. 10.—The verb to *shake* is now seldom used in any other than the irregular form, *shake, shook, shaking, shaken*; and, in this form only, is it recognized by our principal grammarians and lexicographers, except that Johnson improperly acknowledges *shook* as well as *shaken* for the perfect participle: as, "I've *shook* it off."—DRYDEN: *Joh. Dict.* But the regular form, *shake, shaked, shaking, shaked*, appears to have been used by some writers of high reputation; and, if the verb is not now properly redundant, it formerly was so. Examples regular: "The frame and huge foundation of the earth *shak'd* like a coward."—SHAKSPEARE: *Hen. IV.* "I am he that is so *love-shaked.*"—ID.: *As You Like it.* "A sly and constant knave, not to be *shak'd.*"—ID.: *Cymbeline: Joh. Dict.* "I thought he would have *shaked* it off."—TATTLER: *ib.* "To the very point I *shaked* my head at."—*Spectator,* No. 4. "From the ruin'd roof of *shak'd* Olympus."—*Milton's Poems.* "None hath *shak'd* it off."—*Walker's English Particles,* p. 89. "They *shaked* their heads."—*Psalms,* cix, 25. Dr. Crombie says, "Story, in his Grammar, has, *most unwarrantably,* asserted, that the Participle of this Verb should be *shaked.*"—ON ETYMOLOGY AND SYNTAX, p. 198. Fowle, on the contrary, pronounces *shaked* to be right. See *True English Gram.,* p. 46.

OBS. 11.—All former lists of our irregular and redundant verbs are, in many respects, defective and erroneous; nor is it claimed for those which are here presented, that they are absolutely perfect. I trust, however, they are much nearer to perfection, than are any earlier ones. Among the many individuals who have published schemes of these verbs, none have been more respected and followed than Lowth, Murray, and Crombie; yet are these authors' lists severally faulty in respect to as many as sixty or seventy of the words in question, though the whole number but little exceeds two hundred, and is commonly reckoned less than one hundred and eighty. By Lowth, eight verbs are made redundant, which I think are now regular only: namely, *bake, climb, fold, help, load, owe, wash.* By Crombie, as many: to wit, *bake, climb, freight, help, lift, load, shape, writhe.* By Murray, two: *load* and *shape.* With Crombie, and in general with the others too, twenty-seven verbs are always irregular, which I think are sometimes regular, and therefore redundant: *abide, beseech, blow, burst, creep, freeze, grind, lade, lay, pay, rive, seethe, shake, show, sleep, slide, speed, string, strive, strow, sweat, thrive, throw, weave, weep, wind, wring.* Again, there are, I think, more than twenty redundant verbs which are treated by Crombie,—and, with one or two exceptions, by Lowth and Murray also,—as if they were always regular: namely, *betide, blend, bless, burn, dive, dream, dress, geld, kneel, lean, leap, learn, mean, mulct, pass, pen, plead, prove, reave, smell, spell, stave, stay, sweep, wake, whet, wont.* Crombie's list contains the auxiliaries, which properly belong to a different table. Erroneous as it is, in all these things, and more, it is introduced by the author with the following praise, in bad English: "*Verbs, which* depart from this rule, are called Irregular, *of which* I believe the subsequent enumeration to be *nearly complete.*"—TREATISE ON ETYM. AND SYNT., p. 192.

OBS. 12.—Dr. Johnson, in his Grammar of the English Tongue, recognizes two forms which would make *teach* and *reach* redundant. But *teached* is now "obsolete," and *rought* is "old," according to his own Dictionary. Of *loaded* and *loaden,* which he gives as participles of *load,* the regular form only appears to be now in good use. For the redundant forms of many words in the foregoing list, as of *abode* or *abided, awaked* or *awoke, besought* or *beseeched, caught* or *catched, hewed* or *hewn, mowed* or *mown, laded* or *laden, seethed* or *sod, sheared* or *shore, sowed* or *sown, waked* or *woke, wove* or *weaved,* his authority may be added to that of others already cited. In Dearborn's Columbian Grammar, published in Boston in 1795, the year in which Lindley Murray's Grammar first appeared in York, no fewer than thirty verbs are made redundant, which are not so represented by Murray. Of these I have retained nineteen in the following list, and left the other eleven to be now considered always regular. The thirty are these: "bake, *bend, build, burn,* climb, *creep, dream,* fold, freight, *geld, heat, heave,* help, *lay, leap,* lift, *light,* melt, owe, *quit,* rent, rot, *seethe, spell, split, strive,* wash, *weave, wet, work.*" See *Dearborn's Gram.,* p. 37-45.


**LIST OF THE REDUNDANT VERBS.**

Imperfect Present. Preterit. Part

Abide, abode *or* abided, abiding, abode *or* abided.
Awake, awaked *or* awoke, awaking, awaked *or* awoke.
Belay, belayed *or* belaid, belaying, belayed *or* belaid.
Bend, bent *or* bended, bending, bent *or* bended.
Bereave, bereft *or* bereaved, bereaving, bereft *or* bereaved.

Beseech, besought *or* beseeched, beseeching, besought *or* beseeched.

Bet, betted *or* bet, betting, betted *or* bet.

Betide, betided *or* betid, betiding, betided *or* betid.

Bide, bode *or* bided, biding, bode *or* bided.

Blend, blended *or* blent, blending, blended *or* blent.

Bless, blessed *or* blest, blessing, blessed *or* blest.

Blow, blew *or* blowed, blowing, blown *or* blowed.

Build, built *or* builded, building, built *or* builded.

Burn, burned *or* burnt, burning, burned *or* burnt.

Burst, burst *or* bursted, bursting, burst *or* bursted.

Catch, caught *or* catched, catching, caught *or* catched.

Clothe, clothed *or* clad, clothing, clothed *or* clad.

Creep, crept *or* creeped, creeping, crept *or* creeped.

Crow, crowed *or* crew, crowing, crowed.

Curse, cursed *or* curst, cursing, cursed *or* curst.

Dare, dared *or* durst, daring, dared.

Deal, dealt *or* dealed, dealing, dealt *or* dealed.

Dig, dug *or* digged, digging, dug *or* digged.

Dive, dived *or* dove, diving, dived *or* diven.

Dream, dreamed *or* dreamt, dreaming, dreamed *or* dreamt.

Dress, dressed *or* drest, dressing, dressed *or* drest.

Dwell, dwelt *or* dwelled, dwelling, dwelt *or* dwelled.

Freeze, froze *or* freezed, freezing, frozen *or* freezed.

Geld, gelded *or* gelt, gelding, gelded *or* gelt.

Gild, gilded *or* gilt, gilding, gilded *or* gilt.

Gird, girded *or* girt, girding, girded *or* girt.

Grave, graved, graving, graved *or* graven.

Grind, ground *or* grinded, grinding, ground *or* grinded.

Hang, hung *or* hanged, hanging, hung *or* hanged.

Heat, heated *or* het, heating, heated *or* het.

Heave, heaved *or* hove, heaving, heaved *or* hoven.

Hew, hewed, hewing, hewed *or* hewn.

Kneel, kneeled *or* knelt, kneeling, kneeled *or* knelt.

Knit, knit *or* knitted, knitting, knit *or* knitted.

Lade, laded, lading, laded *or* laden.

Lay, laid *or* layed, laying, laid *or* layed.

Lean, leaned *or* leant, leaning, leaned *or* leant.

Leap, leaped *or* leapt, leaping, leaped *or* leapt.[292]

Learn, learned *or* learnt, learning, learned *or* learnt.

Light, lighted *or* lit, lighting, lighted *or* lit.

Mean, meant *or* meaned, meaning, meant *or* meaned.

Mow, mowed, mowing, mowed *or* mown.

Mulct, mulcted *or* mulct, mulcting, mulcted *or* mulct.

Pass, passed *or* past, passing, passed *or* past.

Pay, paid *or* payed, paying, paid *or* payed.

Pen, penned *or* pent, penning, penned *or* pent.

 (to coop,)

Plead, pleaded *or* pled, pleading, pleaded *or* pled.

Prove, proved, proving, proved *or* proven.

Quit, quitted *or* quit, quitting, quitted *or* quit.[293]

Rap, rapped *or* rapt, rapping, rapped *or* rapt.

Reave, reft *or* reaved, reaving, reft *or* reaved.

Rive, rived, riving, riven *or* rived.

Roast, roasted *or* roast, roasting, roasted *or* roast.

Saw, sawed, sawing, sawed *or* sawn.

Seethe, seethed *or* sod, seething, seethed *or* sodden.

Shake, shook *or* shaked, shaking, shaken *or* shaked.

Shape, shaped, shaping, shaped *or* shapen.

Shave, shaved, shaving, shaved *or* shaven.

Shear, sheared *or* shore, shearing, sheared *or* shorn.

Shine, shined *or* shone, shining, shined *or* shone.

Show, showed, showing, showed *or* shown.

Sleep, slept *or* sleeped, sleeping, slept *or* sleeped.

Slide, slid *or* slided, sliding, slidden, slid,

                              *or* slided.

Slit, slitted *or* slit, slitting, slitted *or* slit.

Smell, smelled *or* smelt, smelling, smelled *or* smelt.

Sow, sowed, sowing, sowed *or* sown.

Speed, sped *or* speeded, speeding, sped *or* speeded.

Spell, spelled *or* spelt, spelling, spelled *or* spelt.

Spill, spilled *or* spilt, spilling, spilled *or* spilt.

Split, split *or* splitted, splitting, split

                              *or* splitted.[294]

Spoil, spoiled *or* spoilt, spoiling, spoiled *or* spoilt.

Stave, stove *or* staved, staving, stove *or* staved.

Stay, staid *or* stayed, staying, staid *or* stayed.

String, strung *or* stringed, stringing, strung *or* stringed.

Strive, strived *or* strove, striving, strived *or* striven.

Strow, strowed, strowing, strowed *or* strown.

Sweat, sweated *or* sweat, sweating, sweated *or* sweat.

Sweep, swept *or* sweeped, sweeping, swept *or* sweeped.

Swell, swelled, swelling, swelled *or* swollen.

Thrive, thrived *or* throve, thriving, thrived *or* thriven.

Throw, threw *or* throwed, throwing, thrown *or* throwed.

Wake, waked *or* woke, waking, waked *or* woke.

Wax, waxed, waxing, waxed *or* waxen.

Weave, wove *or* weaved, weaving, woven *or* weaved.

Wed, wedded *or* wed, wedding, wedded *or* wed.

Weep, wept *or* weeped, weeping, wept *or* weeped.

Wet, wet *or* wetted, wetting, wet *or* wetted.

Whet, whetted *or* whet, whetting, whetted *or* whet.[295]

Wind, wound *or* winded, winding, wound *or* winded.

Wont, wont *or* wonted, wonting, wont *or* wonted.

Work, worked *or* wrought, working, worked *or* wrought.

Wring, wringed *or* wrung, wringing, wringed *or* wrung.[296]

## DEFECTIVE VERBS.

A *defective verb* is a verb that forms no participles, and is used in but few of the moods and tenses; as, *beware, ought, quoth.*

## OBSERVATIONS.

OBS. 1. When any of the principal parts of a verb are wanting, the tenses usually derived from those parts are also, of course, wanting. All the auxiliaries, except *do, be,* and *have,* if we compare them with other verbs, are defective; but, *as auxiliaries,* they lack nothing; for no complete verb is used throughout as an auxiliary, except *be.* And since an auxiliary differs essentially from a principal verb, the propriety of referring *may, can, must,* and *shall,* to the class of defective verbs, is at least questionable. In parsing there is never any occasion to *call* them defective verbs, because they are always taken together with their principals. And though we may technically say, that their participles are "*wanting,*" it is manifest that none are *needed.*

OBS. 2. *Will* is sometimes used as a principal verb, and as such it is regular and complete; *will, willed, willing, willed*: as, "His Majesty *willed* that they should attend."—*Clarendon.* "He *wills* for them a happiness of a far more exalted and enduring nature."—*Gurney.* "Whether thou *willest* it to be a minister to our pleasure."—*Harris.* "I *will*; be thou clean."—*Luke,* v, 13. "Nevertheless, not as I *will,* but as thou *will.*"—*Matt.,* xxvi, 39. "To *will* is present with me."—*Rom.*, vii, 18. But *would* is sometimes also a principal verb; as, "What *would* this man?"—*Pope.* "Would God that all the Lord's people were prophets."—*Numb.*, xi, 29. "And Israel *would* none of me."—*Psalm*, lxxxi, 11. If we refer this indefinite preterit to the same root, *will* becomes redundant; *will, willed* or *would, willing, willed.* In respect to time, *would* is less definite than *willed*, though both are called preterits. It is common, and perhaps best, to consider them distinct verbs. The latter only can be a participle: as,

"How rarely does it meet with this time's guise,
When man was *will'd* to love his enemies!"—*Shakspeare.*

OBS. 3. The remaining defective verbs are only five or six questionable terms, which our grammarians know not well how else to explain; some of them being now nearly obsolete, and others never having been very proper. *Begone* is a needless coalition of *be* and *gone*, better written separately, unless Dr. Johnson is right in calling the compound an *interjection*: as,

"Begone! the goddess cries with stern disdain,
Begone! nor dare the hallow'd stream to stain!"—*Addison.*

Milton Keynes UK
Ingram Content Group UK Ltd.
UKHW050137080424
440718UK00003B/35